Creating Web Sites

Projects

Carol M. Cram

Meta C. Hirschl

D1399052

ONE MAIN STREET, CAMBRIDGE, MA 02142

COURSE TECHNOLOGY   *an International Thomson Publishing company* I(T)P®

Cambridge • Albany • Bonn • Boston • Cincinnati • London • Madrid • Melbourne • Mexico City
New York • Paris • San Francisco • Singapore • Tokyo • Toronto • Washington

ILLUSTRATED PROJECTS™

COURSE TECHNOLOGY

Creating Web Sites — Illustrated Projects™

is published by Course Technology.

Managing Editor:	Nicole Jones Pinard
Product Manager:	Jeanne Herring
Production Editor:	Daphne Barbas
Development Editor:	Mary-Terese Cozzola
Composition House:	GEX, Inc.
QA Technical Reviewers:	Chris Hall, John McCarthy
Text Designer:	Joseph Lee Design
Cover Designer:	Joseph Lee Design

© 1998 by Course Technology
A Division of International Thomson Publishing —I(T)P®

For more information contact:

Course Technology
One Main Street
Cambridge, MA 02142

International Thomson Publishing Europe
Berkshire House 168-173
High Holborn
London WC1V 7AA
England

Thomas Nelson Australia
102 Dodds Street
South Melbourne, 3205
Victoria, Australia

Nelson Canada
1120 Birchmount Road
Scarborough, Ontario
Canada M1K 5G4

International Thomson Editores
Campos Eliseos 385, Piso 7
Col. Polanco
11560 Mexico D.F. Mexico

International Thomson Publishing GmbH
Königswinterer Strasse 418
53277 Bonn
Germany

International Thomson Publishing Asia
211 Henderson Road
#05-10 Henderson Building
Singapore 0315

International Thomson Publishing Japan
Hirakawacho Kyowa Building, 3F
2-2-1 Hirakawacho
Chiyoda-ku, Tokyo 102
Japan

ISBN 0-7600-5802-4

Printed in the United States of America

10 9 8 7 6 5 4 3

From the Illustrated Series™ Team

At Course Technology we believe that technology will transform the way that people teach and learn. We are very excited about bringing you, instructors and students, the most practical and affordable technology-related products available.

The Development Process
Our development process is unparalleled in the educational publishing industry. Every product we create goes through an exacting process of design, development, review, and testing.

Reviewers give us direction and insight that shape our manuscripts and bring them up to the latest standards. Every manuscript is quality tested. Students whose backgrounds match the intended audience work through every keystroke, carefully checking for clarity and pointing out errors in logic and sequence. Together with our own technical reviewers, these testers help us ensure that everything that carries our name is as error-free and easy to use as possible.

The Products
We show both how and why technology is critical to solving problems in the classroom and in whatever field you choose to teach or pursue. Our time-tested, step-by-step instructions provide unparalleled clarity. Examples and applications are chosen and crafted to motivate students.

The Illustrated Series Team
The Illustrated Series Team is committed to providing you with the most visual introduction to microcomputer applications. No other series of books will get you up to speed faster in today's changing software environment. This book will suit your needs because it was delivered quickly, efficiently, and affordably. In every aspect of business, we rely on a commitment to quality and the use of technology. Each member of the Illustrated Series Team contributes to this process. The names of all our team members are listed below.

Cynthia Anderson	Mary-Terese Cozzola	Meta Chaya Hirschl	Neil Salkind
Chia-Ling Barker	Carol M. Cram	Jane Hosie-Bounar	Gregory Schultz
Donald Barker	Kim T.M. Crowley	Steven Johnson	Ann Shaffer
Ann Barron	Catherine G. DiMassa	Bill Lisowski	Christine Spillett
David Beskeen	Shelley Dyer	Chet Lyskawa	Dan Swanson
Ann Marie Buconjic	Linda Eriksen	Tara O'Keefe	Marie Swanson
Rachel Bunin	Jessica Evans	Harry Phillips	Jennifer Thompson
Joan Carey	Lisa Friedrichsen	Nicole Jones Pinard	Sasha Vodnik
Patrick Carey	Michael Halvorson	Katherine T. Pinard	Jan Weingarten
Sheralyn Carroll	Jeff Goding	Kevin Proot	Christie Williams
Brad Conlin	Jamie Harper	Elizabeth Eisner Reding	Janet Wilson
Pam Conrad	Jeanne Herring	Art Rotberg	

Preface

Welcome to *Creating Web Sites—Illustrated Projects*! This highly visual book offers more than fifty interesting and challenging projects designed to reinforce the skills learned in any book covering beginning Web Site creation skills using Netscape Composer. The Illustrated Projects Series is for people who want more opportunities to practice important software skills.

Organization and Coverage

This text contains a total of six units. Each unit contains three projects, followed by four Independent Challenges and a Visual Workshop. In these units, students practice planning, creating, formatting, and linking Web pages to produce relevant sites such as a personal Web site and a Web site for a small business. The combined purpose of the three projects in each unit is to create one type of Web site.

About this Approach

What makes the Illustrated Projects approach so effective at reinforcing software skills? It's quite simple. Each activity in a project is presented on two facing pages, with the step-by-step instructions on the left page, and large screen illustrations on the right. Students can focus on a single activity without having to turn the page. This unique design makes information extremely accessible and easy to absorb. Students can complete the robust projects on their own and, because of the modular structure of the book, can also cover the units in any order.

The sample two-page spread below highlights the main lesson elements.

Road map—It is always clear which section, project, and activity you are working on.

Introduction—Concise text that introduces the project and explains which activity within the project the student will complete.

Numbered steps—Clear step-by-step directions explain how to complete the specific activity. These steps get less specific as students progress to the third project in a unit.

Hints and Trouble comments—Hints for using the software more effectively and trouble shooting advice to address common problems that might occur. Both appear right where students need them, next to the step where they might need help.

Time To checklists—Reserved for basic skills that students do frequently such as printing, saving, and closing pages.

Web Sites

PROJECT 2

OVERVIEW

Adding Color, Lines, and Images

Once you have developed the *content* of a Web site, you need to add design elements and pictures to make the Web site attractive to readers. Three activities are required to design and enhance Maria Sanchez's personal Web site: Add a Background and Select Text Colors, Insert Horizontal Lines, and Add a Picture and Clip Art.

activity:

Add a Background and Select Text Colors

You need to add a custom background to Maria's Index page, change the text colors, and then add the same background and text colors to the remaining two pages. Your first step is to display the Course Technology Student Online Companion so you can copy the background file to the Index page.

steps:

1. Connect to the Internet if necessary, click the Navigator button on the Components bar, click the Location text box on the Navigator toolbar, type www.course.com, press [Enter], then display the Creating Web Sites Illustrated Projects Student Online Companion

2. Point to <u>unitAback.gif</u>, click the right mouse button, click Save Link As, display the folder containing the files for Maria's Web site, then click Save

Hint
To view the source of the background file, click Credits and Resources at the top of the Creating Web Sites Illustrated Student Online Companion page.

3. Display Maria's Index page, click Format on the menu bar, click Page Colors and Properties, click the Colors and Background tab, then click in the Use Image text box, as shown in Figure P2-1

4. Click Choose File, click <u>unitAback.gif</u>, click Open, then click OK

In a few seconds, the Index page appears with an attractive pink-textured background. Next, you'll center the first two lines of text on the Index page.

5. Select the first two lines of text ("Maria Sanchez" and "Welcome to My Web Site"), click the Alignment button on the Formatting toolbar, click the Center button shown in Figure P2-2, then click away from the selected text

Next, you will change the colors of the normal text and the link text.

Hint
The color of the two links will not change to maroon because they were activated when you checked them in Project 1. The links will appear in maroon when the Web site is published on the World Wide Web.

6. Click Format on the menu bar, click Page Colors and Properties, click the color box next to Normal Text, select the navy box (bottom row, second column from the right), click the blue box next to Link Text, scroll down the list of colors, click the maroon box in the far right column, third row from the bottom, then click OK

Next, you will change the color of the text "Please Go To."

7. Select the text Please Go To:, click the Font Color list arrow on the Formatting toolbar, click the violet box in the far right column, third row from the top, then save the file

You can apply the same background and color scheme to the Resume page and the Skills and Interests page.

8. Display the Resume page, enhance the main headings (e.g., Objective, Education, etc.) and the text Please Go To: with violet, center the text Maria Sanchez, click Format, click Page Colors and Properties, click the Colors and Backgrounds tab if necessary, click in the Use Image text box, click Choose File, click unitAback.gif, click Open, change the Normal Text to navy and the Link Text to maroon, click OK, then click OK

Time To
✓ Print

9. Display the Skills and Interests page, format it with the same custom background and colors, center the text My Skills and My Interests, enhance the subheadings and Please Go To: with violet, save the file, preview the page in Navigator, then close Navigator

The Skills and Interests page appears in Navigator as shown in Figure P2-3. Next, go on to add horizontal lines in selected locations on the three pages.

► WS A-10 CREATING WEB SITES PROJECTS

The Projects

The two-page lesson format featured in this book provides students with a powerful learning experience. However, the projects themselves are the key to the approach. Here are some details:

▶ **Meaningful Examples**—This book features projects that students will be excited to create, including a travel Web site, a community recycling Web site, and a personal Web site. By producing relevant sites that will enhance their own lives, students will more readily master skills.

▶ **Different Levels of Guidance**—The three projects in each unit provide varying levels of guidance. In Project 1, the guidance level is high, with detailed instructions keeping the students on track. Project 2 provides less guidance, and Project 3 provides minimal help, encouraging students to work more independently. This approach gets students in the real-world mindset of using their experiences to solve problems.

▶ **Start from Scratch**—To truly test if a student understands how to create Web pages using Netscape Composer to reach specific goals, the student should start from scratch. This adds to the book's flexibility and real-world nature.

▶ **Outstanding Assessment and Reinforcement**—Each unit concludes with four Independent Challenges. These Independent Challenges offer less instruction than the projects, allowing students to explore various software features and increase their critical thinking skills. Visual Workshops follow the Independent Challenges and broaden students' attention to detail.

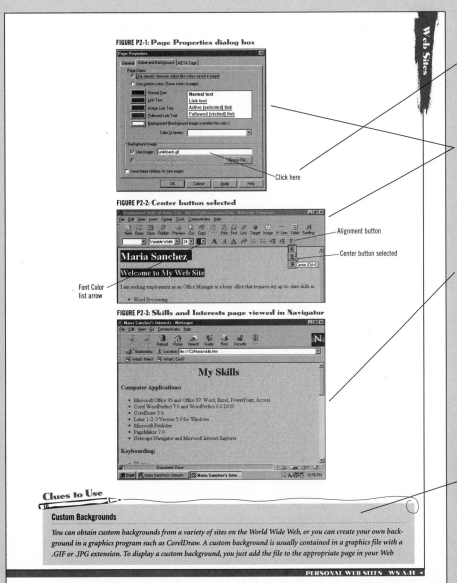

FIGURE P2-1: Page Properties dialog box

FIGURE P2-2: Center button selected

FIGURE P2-3: Skills and Interests page viewed in Navigator

Callouts—The innovative design draws the students' eyes to important areas of the screens.

Screen shots—Every activity features large representations of what the screen should look like as students complete the numbered steps.

Completed screens and documents—Throughout each project, screenshots show students how the project should be developing. At the end of every project, there is a picture of how the project will look when completed. Students can easily assess how well they've done.

Clues to Use boxes—Many activities feature these sidebars, which provide concise information that either explains a skill or concept that is covered in the steps, or describes an independent task or feature that is in some way related to the steps.

Clues to Use

Custom Backgrounds

You can obtain custom backgrounds from a variety of sites on the World Wide Web, or you can create your own background in a graphics program such as CorelDraw. A custom background is usually contained in a graphics file with a .GIF or .JPG extension. To display a custom background, you just add the file to the appropriate page in your Web

Instructor's Resource Kit

The Instructor's Resource Kit is Course Technology's way of putting the resources and information needed to teach and learn effectively into your hands. With an integrated array of teaching and learning tools that offer you and your students a broad range of instructional options, Course Technology provides the highest quality and most cutting-edge resources available to instructors today. These resources can be found at http://www.course.com. Briefly, the resources available with this text are:

Course Faculty Online Companion

This new World Wide Web site offers Course Technology customers a password-protected Faculty Lounge where you can find everything you need to prepare for class. These periodically updated items include lesson plans, graphic files for the figures in the text, additional problems, updates and revisions to the text, links to other Web sites, and access to Student Disk files. This new site is an ongoing project and will continue to evolve throughout the semester. Contact your Customer Service Representative for the site address and password.

Course Student Online Companion

An essential resource for users of this text, the Student Online Companion contains text, images, photos, and links to other sites that students need in order to complete the projects in this book. Students are directed to the Student Online Companion by the steps in a project. The Student Online Companion also contains links to other Course Technology student pages where students can find a graphical glossary of terms found in the text, an archive of meaningful templates, software, hot tips, and Web links to other sites that contain pertinent information. These sites are also ongoing projects and will continue to evolve throughout the semester.

Instructor's Manual

This is quality assurance tested and includes:
- ► *Solutions to end-of-unit material*
- ► *Lecture notes which contain teaching tips from the author*
- ► *Extra Projects*

Clues to Use

The Illustrated Family of Products

This book that you are holding fits into the ILLUSTRATED PROJECTS SERIES—*one series of three in the Illustrated family of products. The other two series are the* ILLUSTRATED SERIES *and the* ILLUSTRATED INTERACTIVE SERIES. *The* ILLUSTRATED SERIES *consists of concepts and applications texts that offer the quickest, most visual way* *to build software skills. The* ILLUSTRATED INTERACTIVE SERIES *is our line of computer-based training multimedia products that offer the novice user a quick, visual and interactive learning experience. All three series are committed to providing you and your students with the most visual and enriching instructional materials.*

► ## Creating Web Sites
Projects

Personal Web Site

In This Unit You Will:

► ## Develop Content

► ## Add Color, Lines, and Images

► ## Create Remote Links and Prepare to Publish

Personal Web sites provide an unparalleled venue for telling the world who you are and what you do. To create a successful personal Web site—one that Web surfers will visit and enjoy—you need to first determine the goal of your site. Do you want to find a job? Share information about a hobby or interest? Promote a product or service? The goal of your Web site determines how you will set up and display the information you want to communicate about yourself. ► In this unit, you will learn how to create a personal Web site for Maria Sanchez, an office manager interested in obtaining employment with a company based in California. The goal of this Web site is to advertise Maria's qualifications to interested employers.

OVERVIEW

Personal Web Site for Maria Sanchez

You need to complete three major tasks in order to set up a personal Web site. First, you need to design the Web site, develop the content, and establish local links between the various pages that make up your site. Second, you need to enhance the Web site with a custom background, font colors, and images so that a visitor to your site can view your information easily and be visually stimulated by the overall design of your site. Finally, you need to publish your Web site on a server and insert remote links to and from other sites on the World Wide Web. You will perform all these tasks by setting up, enhancing, and publishing a personal Web site for Maria Sanchez. Three projects are required to complete Maria's Web site:

Project 1

Developing Content

To develop a Web site for Maria, you first need a *storyboard* for the site. The storyboard consists of a graphic representation of the number of pages in the site and the theme of each page. In Project 1, you will create a Web site that consists of the three pages illustrated in the storyboard in Figure O1-1. The home page, shown as the top page in the figure, introduces readers to the Web site and provides links to the other pages in the site. You will save the home page as index.html. This filename tells the server publishing the Web site that the page is the first and main page in the site. Maria's home page will include her name, her picture, a short description of her career goals, and links to a page showing her resume and a page describing her skills and interests.

Project 2

Adding Colors, Lines, and Images

Once you have gathered all the information for Maria's Web site and established links between the home page and the other two pages, you need to enhance the Web site. You will add a textured background, select new colors for the text, insert horizontal lines, and then add a picture of Maria to the Index page and a clip art image of a runner to her Skills and Interests page. Figure O1-2 illustrates the top portion of the completed Index page as it appears in Netscape Navigator.

Project 3

Creating Remote Links and Publishing

In Project 3 you will create links to Web sites that contain information you want to access often. In addition, you will create an e-mail link so that visitors to Maria's Web site can send messages. Once you've created all the links, you are ready to let the world see your site. The completed Web site exists only as a file stored on your hard or floppy disk until you send it to a Server for publishing on the World Wide Web. You will learn how to publish your Web site with an Internet Service Provider and then add your Web site to a search engine, so that potential employers can find it.

Information Web Site WS D-1

▶ Project 1: **Designing and Creating Frames** WS D-4

▶ Project 2: **Finding and Inserting Health & Fitness Links** WS D-12

▶ Project 3: **Adapting the Site for Frame-Dead Browsers** WS D-16

▶ Independent Challenges WS D-20

▶ Visual Workshop WS D-24

Travel Web Site WS E-1

▶ Project 1: **Creating the Site Framework** WS E-4

▶ Project 2: **Inserting an Image Map and Developing the Kyoto Page** WS E-10

▶ Project 3: **Developing an Online Form** WS E-16

▶ Independent Challenges WS E-20

▶ Visual Workshop WS E-24

Online Business Web Site WS F-1

▶ Project 1: **Building Complex Tables** WS F-4

▶ Project 2: **Creating an Interactive Form with JavaScript** WS F-12

▶ Project 3: **Adding Special Effects with JavaScript** WS F-18

▶ Independent Challenges WS F-20

▶ Visual Workshop WS F-24

Index

INDEX 1

Contents

From the Illustrated Series Team   iii

Preface   iv

Personal Web Site   WS A-1

▸ Project 1: **Developing Content**   WS A-4

▸ Project 2: **Adding Colors, Lines, and Images**   WS A-10

▸ Project 3: **Creating Remote Links and Publishing**   WS A-16

▸ Independent Challenges   WS A-20

▸ Visual Workshop   WS A-24

Small Business Web Site   WS B-1

▸ Project 1: **Developing Content and Design**   WS B-4

▸ Project 2: **Working with Images**   WS B-12

▸ Project 3: **Displaying Alternate Text and Inserting a Counter**   WS B-18

▸ Independent Challenges   WS B-20

▸ Visual Workshop   WS B-24

Community Web Site   WS C-1

▸ Project 1: **Designing and Establishing the Site**   WS C-4

▸ Project 2: **Adding Targets and Visual Excitement**   WS C-12

▸ Project 3: **Expanding the Meta-Information**   WS C-16

▸ Independent Challenges   WS C-20

▸ Visual Workshop   WS C-24

FIGURE 01-1: **Web site storyboard**

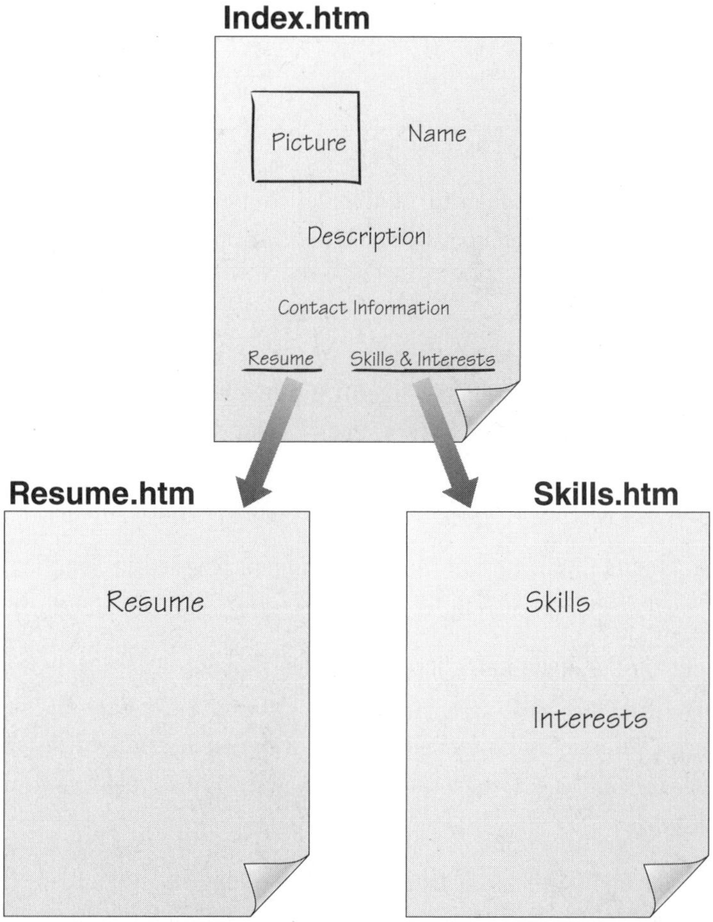

Index.htm

Picture   Name

Description

Contact Information

Resume   Skills & Interests

Resume.htm

Resume

Skills.htm

Skills

Interests

FIGURE 01-2: **Maria's Index page**

DEVELOPING CONTENT

Three activities are required to develop the content for Maria's personal Web site: Set Up the Home Page, Set Up the Resume Page, and Set Up the Skills and Interests Page and Establish Local Links.

activity:

Set Up the Home Page

You first need to create a folder for all the files contained in Maria's Web site and then start Netscape Composer so that you can enter the text that will appear on Maria's home page.

steps:

Hint

Click the Close button on the Components bar, as shown in Figure P1-2, to display it above the taskbar.

Hint

The title on a Web page appears in the title bar of the browser and is used as the name of the page when bookmarked.

1. Start **Windows Explorer**, display the drive where you plan to save all the files for this book, click **File** on the menu bar, point to **New**, click **Folder**, type **Maria**, press **[Enter]**, then close Windows Explorer

   Next, you will open Netscape Composer and then type Maria's name.

2. Start **Netscape Composer**, at the insertion point type **Maria Sanchez**, then press **[Enter]**

   Next, you'll save the page as index.html, so that the server can identify it as the home page for the site.

3. Click **File** on the menu bar, click **Save**, select the **Maria folder**, type **index.html** in the File name text box, then click **Save**

   The Page Title dialog box appears. You need to enter a descriptive title for the Web site because the title will appear in the title bar at the top of the browser. You decide to name the page Employment Skills of Maria Sanchez.

4. Type **Employment Skills of Maria Sanchez** as shown in Figure P1-1, then click **OK**

   Next, you will enhance "Maria Sanchez" with the Heading 1 style.

5. Select the text **Maria Sanchez**, click the **Paragraph Style list arrow** on the Formatting toolbar shown in Figure P1-2, click **Heading 1**, then click after **Sanchez**

   Next, you'll enter a welcome message to Maria's Web site.

6. Press **[Enter]**, type **Welcome to My Web Site**, enhance the line with the **Heading 2 style**, press **[Enter]**, then type the following paragraph of text: **I am seeking employment as an Office Manager in a busy office that requires my up-to-date skills in:**

7. Press **[Enter]** twice, click the **Bullet List button** on the Formatting toolbar, then type the list of skills from **Word Processing** to **Network Administration**, as shown in Figure P1-2

   You can view the page as it will appear in Netscape Navigator or a similar Web browser.

8. Click the **Save button** on the Composition toolbar, then click the **Preview button**

   Your page appears as shown in Figure P1-3. Now you can return to Composer.

9. Click the **Close button** on the Navigator window to return to Composer

Clues to Use

Storing and Saving Web Site Files

You should always store all the files required for a Web site in one folder that contains only the files required for the Web site. By so doing, you simplify the task of transmitting the files to a server for publishing on the World Wide Web. You should also save the files for a Web site in all lowercase letters and add the .HTML extension to the home page to conform to the standard used by most servers for naming files. You can save the other files in a Web site with the default .HTM extension.

FIGURE P1-1: Page Title dialog box

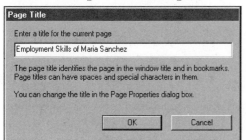

FIGURE P1-2: Completed home page text

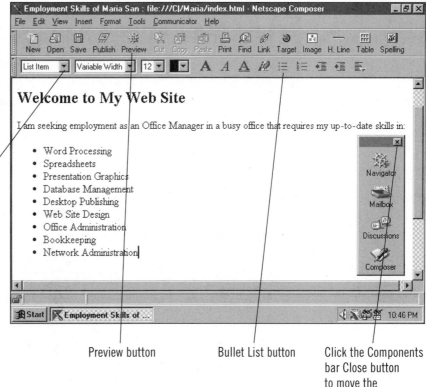

Paragraph Style
list arrow

Preview button

Bullet List button

Click the Components
bar Close button
to move the
Components bar
above the taskbar

FIGURE P1-3: Page viewed in Navigator

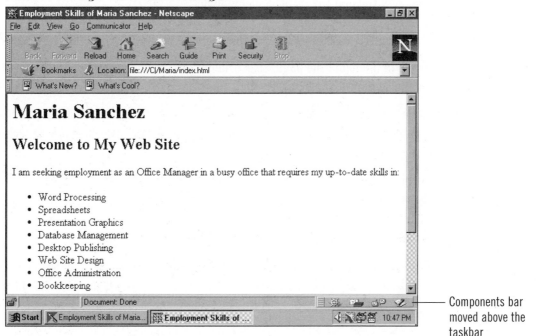

Components bar
moved above the
taskbar

activity:

Set Up the Resume Page

Maria has already created a resume in Microsoft Word. To display the resume in Composer, Maria can simply select all the text in Microsoft Word, copy it, and then paste it into a blank page in Composer. You can copy text from any source into Composer. To obtain the text of Maria's resume, you will open Netscape Navigator, display the Course Technology Student Online Companion, and then copy Maria's resume to a blank page in Composer. You will then enhance the text of the resume with a variety of heading and list styles.

steps:

1. Connect to the Internet, click the **Navigator button** on the Components bar, click the **Location text box** on the Navigator toolbar, type **www.course.com**, press **[Enter]**, scroll down the page that appears, click the **Jump list arrow**, click **Student Online Companions**, click **Creating Web Sites Illustrated Projects**, then under Unit A click **Maria Sanchez's Resume**

2. Click **Edit** on the menu bar, click **Select All**, click **Edit**, click **Copy**, click the **Composer button** on the Components bar, click the **New button** on the Composition toolbar, click **Blank Page**, click **Edit**, then click **Paste**

   Maria's resume appears on a new page in Composer. Next, you will save Maria's resume page.

3. Click **File** on the menu bar, click **Save**, name the file **resume**, click **Save**, type **Maria Sanchez's Resume** over the existing text, then click **OK**

   Next, you will check the page for spelling errors.

4. Scroll to the top of the page, click the **Spelling button** on the Composition toolbar, then make or ignore spelling suggestions as required

   Note that "Sanchez," "Beachside," "Cortez," and "Catalina" are all correctly spelled. Next, you will use heading styles to format Maria's resume attractively.

5. Scroll to the top of the page, select the text **Maria Sanchez**, click the **Paragraph Style list arrow** on the Formatting toolbar, then click **Heading 1**

6. Select the word **Objective**, apply the **Heading 2** style, select the paragraph under "Objective," apply the **Heading 4** style, then apply the **Heading 2** style to **Work Experience** and **Volunteer Experience** as shown in Figure P1-4

7. Scroll to the top of the page, select the text **Administrative Assistant Certificate**, click the **Bold button** on the Formatting toolbar, click the **Italic button**, then apply bold and italics to the remaining job titles as shown in Figure P1-4

   Next, you will enhance selected lists by applying bullets to them.

8. Scroll to the top of the page, select the five items listed under "Courses included," click the **Bullet List button** on the Formatting toolbar, then apply bullets to the remaining lists as shown in Figure P1-4

9. Click the **Save button** on the Composition toolbar, click the **Preview button**, compare your screen with Figure P1-5, close **Navigator**, then click the **Composer button** on the Components bar

   Next, go on to create the Skills and Interests page and then to establish local links between Maria's home page and the other two pages in her Web site.

FIGURE P1-4: Formatted resume

Maria Sanchez

Objective

To apply my organizational and computer skills as an Office Managerin a service-basedcompany or organization

Education

1995 -1996: Beachside College, San Diego, CA
Administrative Assistant Certificate
Courses included:

- Computer Skills: Microsoft Office 95 and 97, WordPerfect 6.0 DOS, Lotus1-2-3 DOS
- Business Communications and Organizational Behavior
- Basic Accounting and Bookkeeping
- Administrative Procedures
- Internet Communications and Web Page Design

1990 -1995: Point Gray Secondary School
Grade 12 Graduation

Work Experience

1996 -1997: West Side Publishing, 1601 Palm Drive, San Diego
Office Manager
Responsibilities included:

- Production of documents with Microsoft Office 97
- Desktop publishing of promotional materials with Microsoft Publisher
- Administration of a six-station Local Area Network
- Design and creation of the company web site
- Organization of office procedures in an eight-person office
- Management of the company database
- Maintenance of financial records

1995-1996: Best Bookkeeping, 3095 West George Street, San Diego
Office Assistant (part-time)

Responsibilities included:

- Maintenance of company records
- Production of documents in Microsoft Word 7.0
- Organization of company database with Microsoft Access 7.0

1991 -1994 Camp Cortez, Catalina Island, CA
Camp Counselor (summers)
Responsibilities included:

- Supervision of groups of 10 campers aged 9 to 11
- Organization of craft and sports activities
- Assistance with general office duties

Volunteer Experience

1993 -1995: Mothers' March, Orange County Chapter
General Office Duties (part-time: January to April)

1995 -1996 Beachside College Applied Business Technology Department
Student Activities Coordinator

FIGURE P1-5: Resume page viewed in Navigator

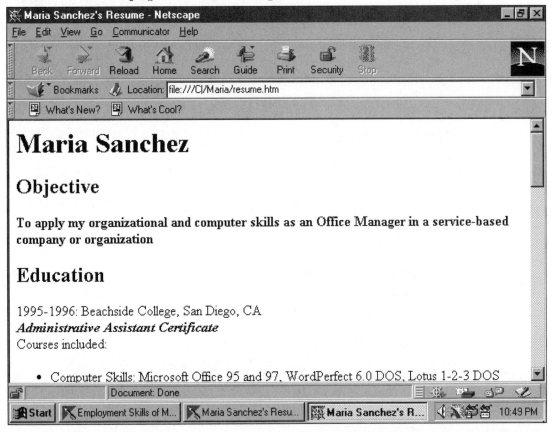

activity:

Set Up the Skills and Interests Page and Establish Local Links

You now need to create the Skills and Interests page. You will enter the text for this page directly into Composer. Then you will create local links between the three pages in Maria's Web site. A *local* link is a link that leads to a page within a Web site. In Project 3, you will learn how to create *remote* links, which send the reader out to other sites on the World Wide Web.

Hint

You can point to a taskbar button to see a ToolTip that shows the entire name of the button.

steps:

1. Click the **New button** on the Composition toolbar, click **Blank Page**, then enter the text and apply heading and bullet styles as shown in Figure P1-6

2. Save the page as **skills.htm**, then enter **Maria Sanchez's Skills and Interests** as the page title
Next, you'll create links between the Index page, the Resume page, and the Skills and Interests page.

3. Click the **Employment Skills button** on the taskbar at the bottom of your screen to display the Index page, scroll to and click at the bottom of the page, press **[Enter]**, click the **Bullet List button** on the Formatting toolbar to remove the bullet, type **Please Go To:**, enhance it with the **Heading 3** style, click at the end of the phrase, then press **[Enter]**

4. Click the **Link button** on the Composition toolbar, in the Link source text box type **Resume**, press **[Tab]**, in the Link to text box type **resume.htm** as shown in Figure P1-7, then click **OK**
"Resume" appears underlined and in purple. Next, you will type the link text and then create the link.

5. Press **[Enter]**, type **Skills and Interests**, select the text you just typed, click, in the Link to area click **Choose File**, in the file list click **skills.htm**, click **Open**, then click **OK**
This link appears underlined and in blue because by creating the link you activated it. Next, you will save the page, and then insert links on the Resume page to Maria's Index page and to her Skills and Interests page. To save time, you will copy the text and links you have just created, paste them to the other pages, and then modify them as necessary.

6. Click the **Save button** on the Composition toolbar, select the three lines from **Please Go To:** through the **Skills and Interests** link, click **Edit** on the menu bar, click **Copy**, display Maria's **Resume page**, scroll to the bottom, press **[Enter]** twice, click **Edit**, then click **Paste**

7. Double-click the **Resume** link to select it, type **Home**, select it, click, in the Link to area click **Choose File**, in the file list click **index.html**, click **Open**, then click **OK**

8. Save the **Resume** page, copy the three lines from **Please Go To:** to the **Skills and Interests** link to the **Skills** page, change the text of the **Skills and Interests** link to **Resume**, modify the link so that it goes to the **resume.htm** file, then save the **Skills and Interests** page
Finally, you'll check the links.

9. Click the **Preview button** on the Composition toolbar, click the **Home** link to display the Index page, scroll to the bottom of the page, click the **Resume** link, then continue to check the links on each of the three pages
As you can see, you can move easily from page to page on Maria's Web site! In Project 2 you will enhance Maria's Web site with a custom background, new text colors, horizontal lines, and two images.

FIGURE P1-6: Text and formatting for the Skills and Interests page

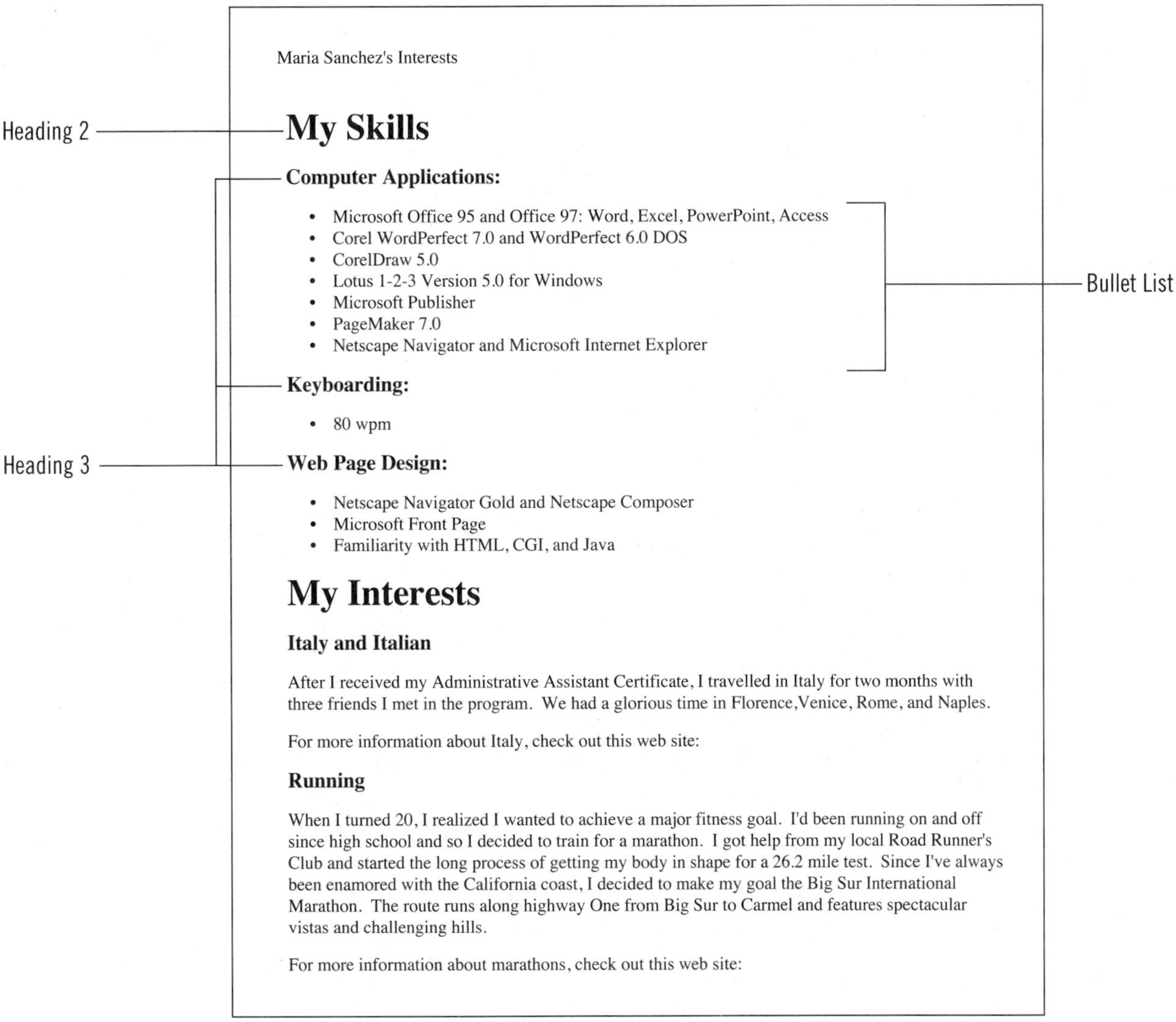

Maria Sanchez's Interests

Heading 2 ———————

My Skills

Computer Applications:

- Microsoft Office 95 and Office 97: Word, Excel, PowerPoint, Access
- Corel WordPerfect 7.0 and WordPerfect 6.0 DOS
- CorelDraw 5.0
- Lotus 1-2-3 Version 5.0 for Windows ——————— Bullet List
- Microsoft Publisher
- PageMaker 7.0
- Netscape Navigator and Microsoft Internet Explorer

Keyboarding:

- 80 wpm

Web Page Design: ——— Heading 3

- Netscape Navigator Gold and Netscape Composer
- Microsoft Front Page
- Familiarity with HTML, CGI, and Java

My Interests

Italy and Italian

After I received my Administrative Assistant Certificate, I travelled in Italy for two months with three friends I met in the program. We had a glorious time in Florence, Venice, Rome, and Naples.

For more information about Italy, check out this web site:

Running

When I turned 20, I realized I wanted to achieve a major fitness goal. I'd been running on and off since high school and so I decided to train for a marathon. I got help from my local Road Runner's Club and started the long process of getting my body in shape for a 26.2 mile test. Since I've always been enamored with the California coast, I decided to make my goal the Big Sur International Marathon. The route runs along highway One from Big Sur to Carmel and features spectacular vistas and challenging hills.

For more information about marathons, check out this web site:

FIGURE P1-7: Character Properties dialog box

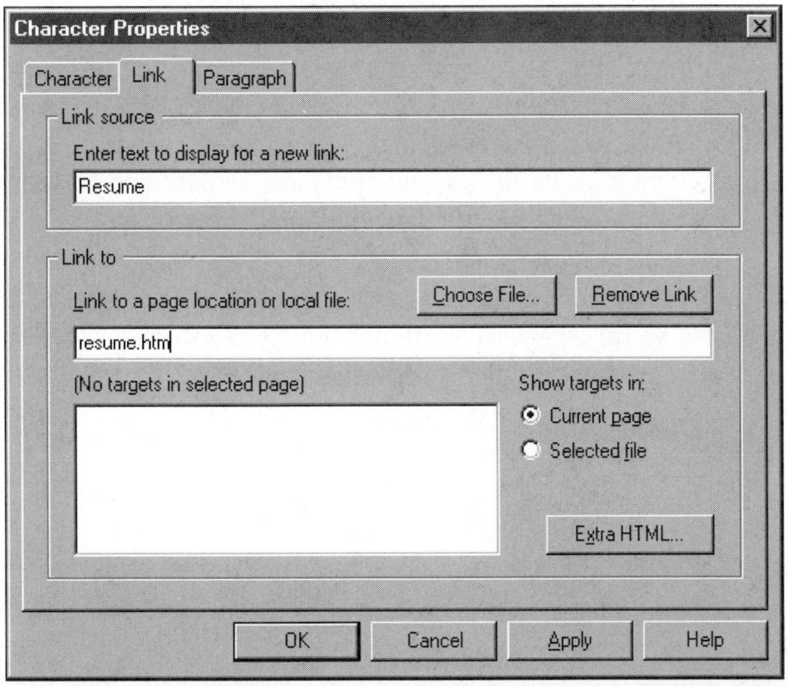

Character Properties [X]

Character | **Link** | Paragraph

Link source

Enter text to display for a new link:

Resume

Link to

Link to a page location or local file: Choose File...   Remove Link

resume.htm

(No targets in selected page)   Show targets in:

◉ Current page
○ Selected file

Extra HTML...

OK   Cancel   Apply   Help

OVERVIEW

Adding Color, Lines, and Images

Once you have developed the *content* of a Web site, you need to add design elements and pictures to make the Web site attractive to readers. Three activities are required to design and enhance Maria Sanchez's personal Web site: **Add a Background and Select Text Colors**, **Insert Horizontal Lines**, and **Add a Picture and Clip Art**.

activity:

Add a Background and Select Text Colors

You need to add a custom background to Maria's Index page, change the text colors, and then add the same background and text colors to the remaining two pages. Your first step is to display the Course Technology Student Online Companion so you can copy the background file to the Index page.

steps:

1. Connect to the Internet if necessary, click the **Navigator button** ⊞ on the Components bar, click the **Location text box** on the Navigator toolbar, type **www.course.com**, press **[Enter]**, then display the **Creating Web Sites Illustrated Projects Student Online Companion**

2. Point to **unitAback.gif**, click the **right mouse button**, click **Save Link As**, display the folder containing the files for Maria's Web site, then click **Save**

3. Display Maria's **Index page**, click **Format** on the menu bar, click **Page Colors and Properties**, click the **Colors and Background tab**, then click in the **Use Image text box**, as shown in Figure P2-1

4. Click **Choose File**, click **unitAback.gif**, click **Open**, then click **OK**

   In a few seconds, the Index page appears with an attractive pink-textured background. Next, you'll center the first two lines of text on the Index page.

5. Select the first two lines of text ("Maria Sanchez" and "Welcome to My Web Site"), click the **Alignment button** 📄 on the Formatting toolbar, click the **Center button** 📄 shown in Figure P2-2, then click away from the selected text

   Next, you will change the colors of the normal text and the link text.

6. Click **Format** on the menu bar, click **Page Colors and Properties**, click the **color box** next to Normal Text, select the **navy box** (bottom row, second column from the right), click the **blue box** next to Link Text, scroll down the list of colors, click the **maroon box** in the far right column, third row from the bottom, then click **OK**

   Next, you will change the color of the text "Please Go To."

7. Select the text **Please Go To:**, click the **Font Color list arrow** on the Formatting toolbar, click the **violet box** in the far right column, third row from the top, then save the file

   You can apply the same background and color scheme to the Resume page and the Skills and Interests page.

8. Display the **Resume** page, enhance the main headings (e.g., **Objective**, **Education**, etc.) and the text **Please Go To:** with **violet**, center the text **Maria Sanchez**, click **Format**, click **Page Colors and Properties**, click the **Colors and Backgrounds tab** if necessary, click in the **Use Image text box**, click **Choose File**, click **unitAback.gif**, click **Open**, change the Normal Text to **navy** and the Link Text to **maroon**, click **OK**, then click **OK**

9. Display the **Skills and Interests** page, format it with the same custom background and colors, center the text **My Skills** and **My Interests**, enhance the subheadings and **Please Go To:** with **violet**, save the file, preview the page in Navigator, then close Navigator

   The Skills and Interests page appears in Navigator as shown in Figure P2-3. Next, go on to add horizontal lines in selected locations on the three pages.

Hint

To view the source of the background file, click Credits and Resources at the top of the Creating Web Sites Illustrated Student Online Companion page.

Hint

The color of the two links will not change to maroon because they were activated when you checked them in Project 1. The links will appear in maroon when the Web site is published on the World Wide Web.

FIGURE P2-1: Page Properties dialog box

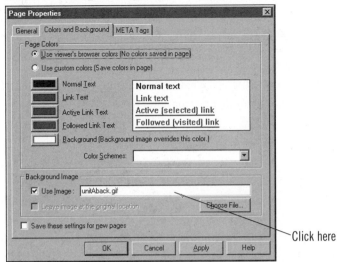

FIGURE P2-2: Center button selected

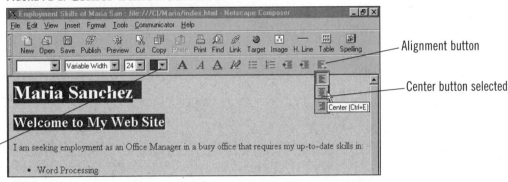

FIGURE P2-3: Skills and Interests page viewed in Navigator

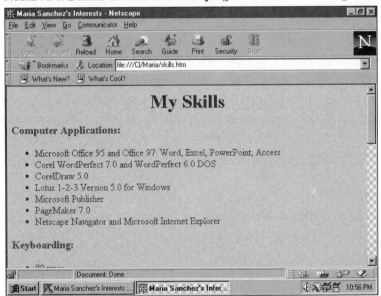

Clues to Use

Custom Backgrounds

You can obtain custom backgrounds from a variety of sites on the World Wide Web, or you can create your own background in a graphics program such as CorelDraw. A custom background is usually contained in a graphics file with a .GIF or .JPG extension. To display a custom background, you just add the file to the appropriate page in your Web

activity:

Insert Horizontal Lines

You insert horizontal lines to separate information in a Web page. Strategically placed horizontal lines help to break up the space and focus the reader's attention. You need to insert horizontal lines on each page of Maria's Web site to separate information.

steps:

1. Display the **Index** page, click after **Welcome to My Web Site**, then press **[Enter]**

   Next, you will insert a horizontal line to separate the two heading lines from the first paragraph of text.

2. Click the **H. Line button** ⬜ on the Composition toolbar

   Next, you want to modify the horizontal line.

3. **Right-click** the horizontal line, click **Horizontal Line Properties**, change the height to **4** pixels, make sure that the **3-D shading check box** is selected as shown in Figure P2-4, then click **OK**

4. Scroll down the page, click to the left of **Please Go To;**, press **[Enter]**, press **[Up Arrow]**, then click ⬜

   Note that the line appears with the settings you specified in Step 3.

5. Save the file, then click the **Preview button** ⬜ on the Composition toolbar

   A preview of the Index page appears as shown in Figure P2-5. Next, you'll add horizontal lines to the Resume page.

6. Display the **Resume** page, click to the left of **Objective**, then click ⬜

7. Insert horizontal lines above **Education**, **Work Experience**, **Volunteer Experience**, and **Please Go To:**, then save the file

8. Display the **Skills and Interests page**, click to the right of the text **My Skills**, insert a horizontal line, click to the right of **My Interests**, insert a horizontal line, click to the left of **Please Go To:**, insert a horizontal line, then save the page

9. Preview the **Skills and Interests** page in Navigator, click the **Resume** link, compare your page with Figure P2-6, then close all the Navigator windows currently active

   Next, you want to insert a picture of Maria on the Index page and a clip art image on the Skills and Interests page.

Hint

Click to the left of each heading, then click the H. Line button so that each line appears in the same place with relation to each heading. To remove a line, click on it and press [Delete].

Clues to Use

Close Windows to Save Space

You should frequently "clean up" your system by closing Navigator windows that you are no longer using. By so doing, you reduce the amount of memory your computer requires.

FIGURE P2-4: Horizontal Line Properties dialog box

Line height changed to 4 pixels

3-D shading selected

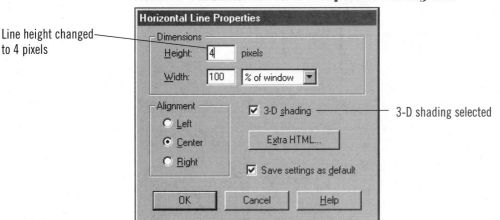

FIGURE P2-5: Index page viewed in Navigator

FIGURE P2-6: Resume page viewed in Navigator

activity:

Add a Picture and Clip Art

If you have a scanner or a digital camera, you can turn pictures into files that you can then display on your Web site. If you work with a graphics program such as CorelDraw, you can create your own pictures or you can insert clip art pictures from any program into a graphics program and save them as .JPG files. Note that images you wish to display in a Web page should be saved in either a .JPG or .GIF format. Your first step is to display the Course Technology Student Online Companion so you can copy a picture of Maria Sanchez to the Index page.

Hint

To view the source of Maria's picture, click Credits and Resources at the top of the Creating Web Sites Illustrated Student Online Companion page.

steps:

1. Display the **Creating Web Sites Illustrated Projects Student Online Companion**, point to **maria.jpg**, click the **right mouse button**, click **Save Link**, open the **Maria folder**, then click **Save**

2. Display the **Index** page, click after **Welcome to My Web Site**, press **[Enter]**, then click the **Insert Image button** on the Composition toolbar

3. Click **Choose File**, display Maria's folder if necessary, click **maria.jpg**, click **Open**, then click **OK**
   A large picture of Maria appears. You need to reduce the size of the image and then position it.

4. Click the image, move your mouse over the top right corner to display the sizing arrows, then click and drag the arrows down to the bottom of the screen

Hint

Drag the horizontal scroll bar at the bottom of your screen to the left so that you can see where the image appears with relation to the left margin of the page. You will need to drag the image a few times before the size is correct.

5. Click the image again, reduce its size so that it appears as shown in Figure P2-7, then save the file
   Next, you will insert a clip art image of a runner on the Skills and Interests page.

6. Display the **Creating Web Sites Illustrated Projects Student Online Companion**, right-click **running.jpg**, click **Save Link**, open the **Maria folder**, then click **Save**

7. Display the **Skills and Interests** page, click at the beginning of the paragraph under "Running", click , select **running.JPG**, click **Open**, click **OK**, then resize the image so that it appears as shown in Figure P2-8
   You've decided that you'd like the text about Maria's running activities to appear alongside the clip art image.

8. Right-click the image, click **Image Properties**, click the **wrapping style icon** as shown in Figure P2-9, click **OK**, then save the file
   You can only see wrapped text in Navigator, so you need to preview the Skills and Interests page now.

9. Click the **Preview button** on the Composition toolbar, scroll down the page to see how the text appears next to the clip art image, then close Navigator
   Next, go on to Project 3, where you will learn how to publish Maria's personal Web site, add remote links, and add Maria's site to a variety of search engines.

FIGURE P2-7: Picture of Maria resized

Insert Image button

Drag the horizontal scroll bar to the left

FIGURE P2-8: Running clip art resized

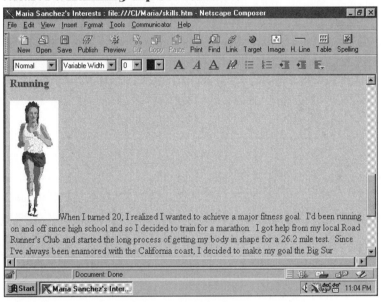

FIGURE P2-9: Image Properties dialog box

Wrapping Style option selected

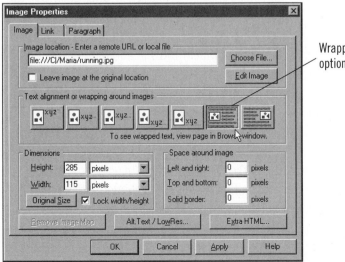

Creating Remote Links and Publishing

You have decided to insert several remote links in Maria's Skills and Interests page to point readers to other sites on the World Wide Web. In addition, you will insert links to help Maria in her job search efforts. While the World Wide Web is an excellent resource for job hunting, you realize that Maria will need to continually check on the market. By adding links to Web sites that post information about potential employers and jobs, Maria can easily visit the sites any time she visits her own home page.

activity:

Create Remote Links

steps:

1. Display the **Skills and Interests** page, scroll to the bottom of the page and click after the last bulleted item, press [Enter], click the **Bullet List button** on the Composition toolbar to remove the bullet, type **Use the following links to search for employment in California:**, apply the **Heading 3 style** to the text, save the file, then click the **Navigator button** on the Components bar

    You will first browse for a good employment Web site and then copy the link to the page.

2. Connect to the Internet, if necessary, click the **Search button** on the Navigation toolbar, scroll down the page, then click <u>AltaVista</u>, as shown in Figure P3-1

    Next, you will type the search criteria.

3. Click in the **Search text box** on the Alta Vista page, type **jobs AND seeking**, press [Enter], scroll down the results, click <u>CONNECT Job Placement Information for Student Services</u>, click <u>Job Boards</u>, then click <u>State Job Boards</u>, or if you cannot locate the site, display the **Creating Web Sites Illustrated Projects Student Online Companion** and click <u>California Jobs</u> under Unit A

    This Web page is a good resource for finding employment, so in addition to copying the URL to the Skills and Interests page, you will also bookmark it.

4. Click the **Bookmarks button** on the Location toolbar, click **Add Bookmark**, then click in the **Location text box** and press [Ctrl][C]

5. Return to the **Skills and Interests** page, click just below **Use the following links to search for employment in California:**, press [Ctrl][V], select the URL, click the **Link button** on the Composition toolbar, press [Ctrl][V] again to paste the URL in the Link to a page location or local file text box, then click **OK**

6. Use Alta Vista to find two more employment URLs to add to the Skills and Interests page, save the page, then preview the page in Navigator

    Compare your screen with P3-2. Note that the URLs you find might be different from the ones displayed in Figure P3-2.

7. Display the **Skills and Interests** page in Composer, scroll to **My Interests**, click after **For more information about Italy, check out this Web site:**, then type **Cool Italian Travel Site**

8. Display Navigator, click **File** on the menu bar, click **Open Page**, type **yahoo.com**, click **Open**, click <u>Countries</u>, click <u>Italy</u>, find a site that provides travel information about Italy, copy the URL, return to the Skills and Interests page in Composer, select the text **Cool Italian Travel Site**, make a link, paste the URL in the Link to text box, then save the page, and close any open windows

9. Add a cool site about marathons to the Running area, save the page, display it in Navigator, compare your screen with Figure P3-3, test all the remote links, then close Navigator

Hint

After testing a remote link, close the Navigator window, return to Composer, then click the Preview button on the Composition toolbar to view the next link. By so doing, you avoid opening several Navigator windows at once.

Hint

Try searching for running AND marathons in Excite.

FIGURE P3-1: Net Search

Click for Alta Vista Search page

FIGURE P3-2: Links to employment sites

Your links might differ

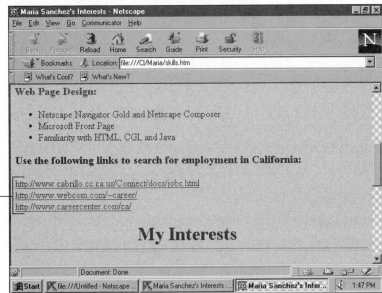

FIGURE P3-3: Links to Italy and marathon sites

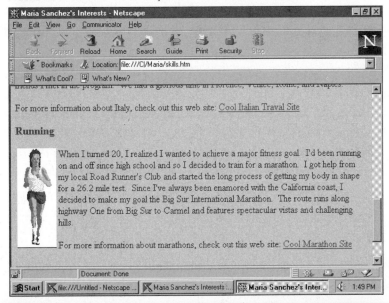

Web Sites

activity:

Adding an E-mail Link and Publishing the Web Site

Before you publish the Web site on the World Wide Web, you need to provide an easy way for visitors to send e-mail. On Maria's site, you will add a link that opens a mail message composition window that is already addressed to Maria. Once you have completed a Web site, the next step is to publish it with an Internet Service Provider (or ISP). The ISP provides a server that hosts your site and makes it available to World Wide Web users. Once the site is available on an ISP, Maria will need to add it to one or more search engines, so that people can find it. You will not publish Maria's Web site in this activity, but you will learn about the publishing process and how to add the site to a search engine.

steps:

1. Display the **Index** page in Composer, scroll to and click at the bottom of the page, press **[Enter]**, type **To Contact Me Directly:**, select the text, apply the **Heading 3 style**, deselect the text, then press **[Enter]**

   Next, you will create a link that allows readers to send Maria e-mail.

2. Type **msanchez@edu.com**, select it, click the **Link button** on the Composition toolbar, in the Link to a page location or local file text box type **mailto:msanchez@edu.com**, then click **OK**

   Now readers can simply click the e-mail link and type their message. Next, you learn how to publish Maria's Web site on the World Wide Web.

Hint

When you publish a Web page, you add meta-information. You'll learn more about this in a later unit.

3. Click the **Publish button** on the Composition toolbar, then click in the **HTTP or FTP Location to publish to list box** as shown in Figure P3-4

   Note that you should always publish from the Index page.

4. Type the HTTP or FTP location that is supplied by your instructor, then click **OK**

   For the purposes of this example, a sample FTP location has been entered.

5. Click the **Navigator button** on the Components bar, click **File** on the menu bar, click **Open Page**, type in the URL assigned to your Web site, then preview the home page in Navigator

   Note that each ISP will provide a different URL, depending on the environment and whether you choose to pay for an easy-to-use URL.

   Next, you will learn how to add Maria's site to the Yahoo search engine.

6. Connect to the Internet if necessary, click **File** on the menu bar, click **Open Page**, type **www.yahoo.com**, click <u>**How to Include Your Site**</u>, then read the instructions about adding your site to Yahoo

   When you add a site to Yahoo, you must specify the category.

7. Click the **Back button** to return to the Yahoo home page, click <u>**Companies**</u>, under Companies click <u>**Office Supplies and Services**</u>, click <u>**Administrative Support**</u>, click <u>**Employment**</u>, click <u>**Individual Resumes**</u>, then click **Add URL** in the page banner as shown in Figure P3-5

   You will fill in the form as if you were going to send it. However, since this is a fictitious resume, you won't submit it.

8. Scroll to the form and fill in the information for Maria as shown in Figure P3-6, then click <u>**Other places**</u> at the bottom of the page and follow any links of interest to learn more about other submission options

9. Close Netscape without submitting the form, disconnect from the Internet, then exit Netscape Communicator

FIGURE P3-4: Publish dialog box

Publish: C:\Maria\index.html

Page Title: [ployment Skills of Maria Sanchez] e.g.: "My Web Page"

HTML Filename: [index.html] e.g.: "mypage.htm"

HTTP or FTP Location to publish to:
[http://www.publishit.com ▼]

User name: [Maria Sanchez]   [Use Default Location]

Password: [*******]   ☐ Save password

Other files to include
⦿ Files associated with this page   ○ All files in page's folder

[Select None] file:///C|/Maria/maria.jpg
               file:///D|/Maria/UnitABack.gif
[Select All]

[OK]   [Cancel]   [Help]

FIGURE P3-5: Yahoo banner

Click here to add URL

FIGURE P3-6: Add to Yahoo

Name:	Maria Sanchez
Email:	msanchez@edu.com
Phone:	614-555-4717
Fax:	614-555-4718
Address:	1001 Monterey Bay
City:	San Diego
State/Province:	CA
Postal Code:	21110
Country:	USA

Document: Done

🏁 Start | file:///Untitled - Netscape... | Maria Sanchez's Interests :... | Add to Yahoo - Nets... | 4:36 PM

Clues to Use

Finding an Internet Service Provider

You can choose from a variety of ISP options, including commercial providers such as America Online and CompuServe, both of which provide space on their servers for customers' Web sites, or a local ISP that offers services depending on whether your site is commercial, personal, or educational. You could even build your own Web server! You might have an ISP available in your lab environment. Check with your instructor or network administrator to find the ISP available for your use with this textbook. When you are looking for an ISP, you might want to consider these questions: Will you pay a flat monthly fee, or is connect time also charged? Does your ISP give you space for publishing your own Web site? How much space are you given on the server and what is the cost? What is the speed of your modem and will the ISP support it? Does the ISP offer you an e-mail address and if so, what is the cost? Check with each local ISP to compare the facts.

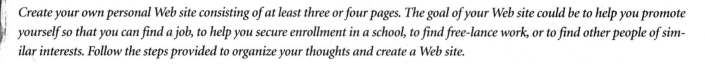

Independent Challenges

INDEPENDENT CHALLENGE 1

Create your own personal Web site consisting of at least three or four pages. The goal of your Web site could be to help you promote yourself so that you can find a job, to help you secure enrollment in a school, to find free-lance work, or to find other people of similar interests. Follow the steps provided to organize your thoughts and create a Web site.

1. Fill in the box below with the goal of your Web site:

The goal of my Web site is to:

2. Determine the purpose of each page in your Web site. Use the table below to organize your site.

Page Content	Filename
Introduce yourself and provide links to other sites.	index.html

3. Use the chart below to define the structure of your Web site. You might need to modify it to match your needs.

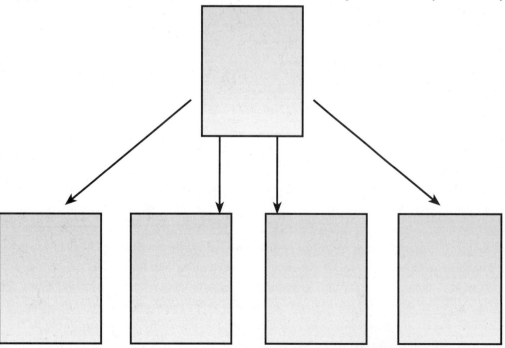

4. Create a folder called "My Personal Site." You will save all the files associated with your personal Web site to this folder.

5. Display Netscape Composer and create the contents for each of the pages.

6. Add local links between the pages. Remember that you should be able to return to the Index page from every page in your Web site. You should also be able to link to every other page in the site from any page. View the pages in your Web site in Navigator, and check each link and page.

INDEPENDENT CHALLENGE 2

Add a custom background and modify the text colors, and then add images and horizontal lines to the pages in your Web site. Be sure to determine a consistent look for all the pages so that the site is visually coherent.

1. Fill in the following table:

Background to use:

To find a selection of custom backgrounds, click Credits and Resources in the Creating Web Sites Illustrated Projects Student Online Companion

Color to use for type: ....

What element(s) do I want to emphasize? ....

What design elements will I use? (e.g. lines, clip art, photos) ....

2. Display Netscape Composer, and based on the table in Step 2, add colors, horizontal lines, clip art, and photographs.

3. View each page in Navigator to check the appearance. Save all the pages.

INDEPENDENT CHALLENGE 3

Add a link to your e-mail address, add remote links, publish your personal Web site, and add your Web site to a search engine.

1. Create a link to your e-mail address from an appropriate location on the Index page. Remember to type "mailto" before your e-mail address in the Link to text box. Here's an example of a correct entry: mailto:jjones@direct.uk.

2. Connect to the Internet and search for relevant Web sites that you can add as remote links to your personal Web site. For example, you might want to find free-lance opportunities in your state or province, or you might want to find universities that offer electronic submission of applications, or you might want to find discussion groups that are relevant to your interests.

3. When you find Web sites that you want to include as links, select the URL, press [Ctrl][C], go to your Web page in Composer, then press [Ctrl][V]. Select the text and make it a link. Repeat this method to insert each of the remote links.

4. Print a copy of the pages in your Web site. To print a page, click File on the menu bar, click Page Setup, make sure the Black Text check box is selected, click OK, then click Print this Page. Note that you will need to print each page separately.

5. Publish your Web site to the ISP available to you. Be sure to put the correct URL in the Publish dialog box.

6. Add your Web site to at least two search engines. You can begin with Yahoo! and then add your site to other engines such as AltaVista and WebCrawler.

7. Disconnect from the Internet and exit Netscape Communicator.

INDEPENDENT CHALLENGE 4

You've been asked to design and create a Web site for a family reunion that will include your extended family around the world. You will include all the information about the reunion, plus fun photographs of family members.

1. Determine the content of each page in your Web site. For example, one page could give directions to the various festivities; one page could provide hotel information; one page could provide activities information; one page could include a family tree with addresses, phone numbers, e-mail addresses, and Web site URLs of each family member involved in the reunion; and one page could display photographs of various family members.

Complete the table below with a brief description of the contents of each page in the Web site and the filenames you will use.

Page Name	Content	Filename
Home page	Welcome the family members to the Web site. Briefly describe the event.	index.html
Page 1		
Page 2		
Page 3		
Page 4		
Page 5		

2. Create a folder called "Reunion" for the contents of the Web site.

3. Display Netscape Composer and create the content for the pages and local links.

4. Test all the links and view the pages in Navigator.

5. Enhance the appearance of the pages with a background and new font colors, and apply appropriate styles to selected text.

6. Insert photographs of family events and family members. Remember you can scan photographs at many copy shops for a fee.

7. Create links to other family members' Web sites. Create an e-mail link that users can click to send you e-mail.

8. Connect to the Internet and search on the World Wide Web for tourist information and maps for the location of the reunion. An example of a map of Paris is shown in the figure below. Create links on your site to the maps and tourist information you found.

FIGURE IC-1: Interactive map of Paris

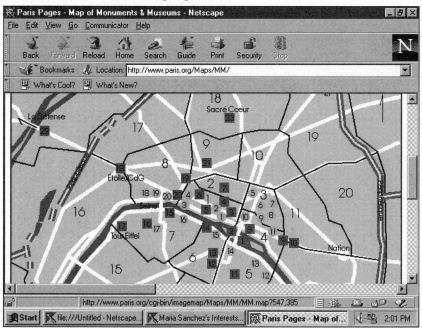

9. View your Web site and test all links, both local and remote.

10. Publish your Web site to the Internet Service Provider (ISP) of your choice.

11. Add your Web site to at least one search engine.

12. Save all the pages, print them, disconnect from the Internet, then exit Netscape Communicator.

Visual Workshop

Create a folder called "Workshop," and then create the Web page shown in Figure VW-1 below, and save it as italy.htm. You will find the background texture (bkgrnd2.gif) and the image (hadrian.jpg) listed under Unit A on the Creating Web Sites Illustrated Projects Student Online Companion (www.course.com, Student Online Companions). Create a link to information about Hadrian's Villa (search for Hadrian AND Villa in Excite, and then click Site 11: Hadrian's Villa or copy the link displayed as More pictures of Hadrian's Villa on the Creating Web Sites Illustrated Projects Student Online Companion). Display the normal text in yellow, the link text in dark blue green, and the followed link text in dull dark blue. When you have completed the page, view it in Navigator, compare it with Figure VW-2 below, and then print a copy. (*Hint*: Select Black Text in the Page Setup dialog box before printing the page.)

FIGURE VW-1: Italy page in Composer

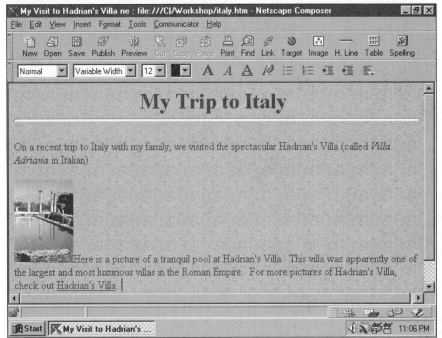

FIGURE VW-2: Italy page previewed in Navigator

► Creating Web Sites
Projects

Small Business Web Site

In This Unit You Will:

► Develop Content and Design

► Work with Images

► Display Alternate Text and Insert a Counter

More and more small businesses are recognizing the advertising potential of the World Wide Web. For less than the cost of a typical Yellow Pages advertisement, businesses can advertise their products and services to millions—not thousands—of potential customers. While sales might not directly increase as a result of exposure on the World Wide Web, the *visibility* of a company increases many-fold, which can, in the long run, result in a larger customer base. A small business can choose to use the World Wide Web simply as an advertising medium, or it can choose to sell its products and services online. ► In this unit you will learn how to create a Web site to advertise the services offered by Tranquility Landscaping, a small landscaping business based in North Vancouver, British Columbia. Tranquility Landscaping is not set up to sell its services online, so its goal is to establish a presence on the World Wide Web that will keep current and future customers informed about the business.

OVERVIEW

Tranquility Landscaping Web Site

The Web site you will develop for Tranquility Landscaping will inform current and potential customers about the company and also enable them to e-mail the company directly. Figure O1-1 illustrates the storyboard for Tranquility Landscaping. Five pages are required for the site: the home page, a page that describes maintenance services, a page that describes garden design services, a page that describes a variety of planting options, and a page that introduces the personnel at Tranquility Landscaping. Three projects are required to build the Web site for Tranquility Landscaping.

Project 1

Developing Content and Design

In Project 1, you will first establish an overall design for the Web site. You will select a background image and font colors for the home page and then create a table of contents that contains links to each of the four other pages in the Web site. When you design a Web site, you want to minimize repetitive tasks. To save time, therefore, you will apply the background and font colors to the home page and create a heading, save the home page as index.html, and then save the page four more times as each of the four filenames you've selected: mainten.htm, design.htm, planting.htm, and person.htm. You will then have the framework for the five pages that make up the Web site, each page with the same background, font colors, and heading text. You can then go on to establish the local links and enter the text required for each page.

Project 2

Working with Images

You will first display the index.html file and insert images that you will designate as links. Figure O1-2 displays a portion of the completed index.html page for Tranquility Landscaping viewed in Navigator. Next, you will start the Windows 95 Paint program and add text to an image. Finally, you will insert the modified image and two more images on the design.htm page.

Project 3

Displaying Alternate Text and Inserting a Counter

In Project 3, you will insert an image with alternate text and an alternate low-resolution image on the planting.htm page. You will then learn how to contact your server so that you can insert a counter on the index.html page to record how many users have visited the Tranquility Landscaping Web site.

FIGURE 01-1: Web site storyboard

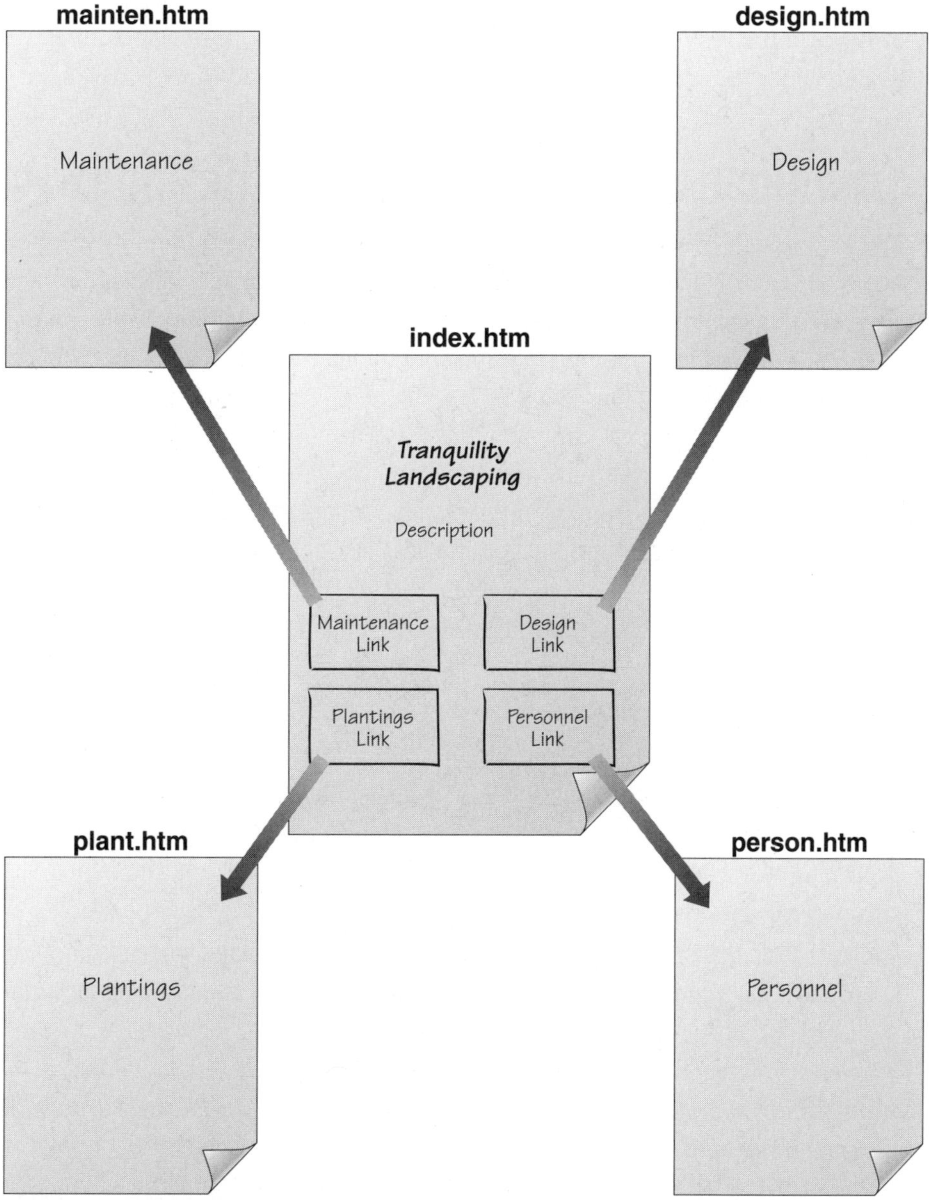

mainten.htm

Maintenance

design.htm

Design

index.htm

*Tranquility
Landscaping*

Description

Maintenance
Link

Design
Link

Plantings
Link

Personnel
Link

plant.htm

Plantings

person.htm

Personnel

FIGURE 01-2: Tranquility Landscaping Index page

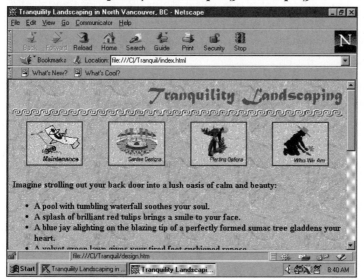

DEVELOPING CONTENT AND DESIGN

Four activities are required to develop the design and content for Tranquility Landscaping's Web site: **Download Images and Set Up the Index Page**, **Create the Table of Contents**, **Develop the Index and Maintenance Pages**, and **Develop the Design, Planting, and Who We Are Pages**.

activity:

Download Images and Set Up the Index Page

You first need to create a folder for all the files contained in the Tranquility Landscaping Web site and access the Course Technology Student Online Companion. You will then download the images you need to complete Project 1, insert the background image you wish to display on each of the five pages in the site, and create a heading that includes the name of the company (Tranquility Landscaping) and a custom horizontal line.

steps:

Hint

Click the Close button on the Components bar to move it to the bottom of the screen.

Hint

If the Page Title dialog box does not appear, click Format, click Page Colors and Properties, click the General tab, enter the title of the page, then click OK.

1. Create a folder called **Tranquil** in the directory where you store your files for this book, connect to the Internet, start **Netscape Navigator**, click the **Location text box** on the Navigator toolbar, type **www.course.com**, press **[Enter]**, click **Download**, scroll down the page that appears, click **Student Online Companions**, click **Creating Web Sites Illustrated Projects**, point to **unitBback.jpg**, click the **right mouse button**, click **Save Link As**, display the **Tranquil folder**, then click **Save**

2. Repeat the save procedure to save the files **line1.gif**, **tranquil.htm**, and **star.gif** to the **Tranquil folder**
   Next, you will insert the unitBback.jpg image as the background.

3. Click the **Composer button** on the Components bar to display a blank page in Composer, click **Format** on the menu bar, click **Page Colors and Properties**, click the **Colors and Background tab**, click **Choose File**, open the **Tranquil folder**, click **unitBback.jpg**, click **Open**, then click **OK**
   Next, you will save the page as index.html.

4. Click **File** on the menu bar, click **Save**, select the **Tranquil folder**, type **index.html** in the File name text box, click **Save**, in the Page Title dialog box type **Tranquility Landscaping in North Vancouver, BC** as shown in Figure P1-1, then click **OK**
   You assign the name "index" and the extension ".html" to the first page in a Web site so that the server can identify the page as the home page for the site. Next, you will enter "Tranquility Landscaping" at the right side of the screen.

5. Press **[Ctrl][R]** to turn on right alignment, type **Tranquility Landscaping**, then press **[Enter]**
   Next, you will change the font style, font size, and color of "Tranquility Landscaping."

6. Select the text, click the **Font list arrow**, select **Matura MT Script Capitals** if available, or select another script-like font, click the **Font Size list arrow**, click **24**, click the **Color list arrow**, click **Other**, click the **teal box** in the third row, fourth column, then click **OK**
   Next, you will insert the line1.gif image.

7. Click to the right of the text, press **[Enter]**, click the **Image button** on the Composition toolbar, click **Choose File**, click **line1.gif**, click **Open**, then click **OK**
   You need to display the Image Properties box so you can adjust the height and width of the line.

8. Right-click the **line**, click **Image Properties**, double-click in the **Height text box**, type **5**, click the **list arrow** next to **pixels**, select **% of window**, double-click in the **Width text box**, type **100**, click the **list arrow** next to **pixels**, select **% of window**, compare your Image Properties dialog box with Figure P1-2, then click **OK**

9. Click at the right end of the line, press **[Enter]**, press **[Ctrl][L]** to return the insertion point to the left margin, click the **Preview button** on the Composition toolbar, click **Yes** to save the page, compare your screen with Figure P1-3, then close Navigator
   Next, go on to create the remaining four pages in the Web site and then to create the table of contents.

FIGURE P1-1: Page Title dialog box

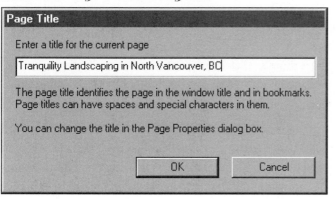

FIGURE P1-2: Image Properties dialog box

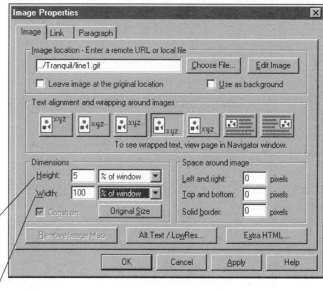

Height changed to 5% of window

Width changed to 100% of window

FIGURE P1-3: Index page viewed in Navigator

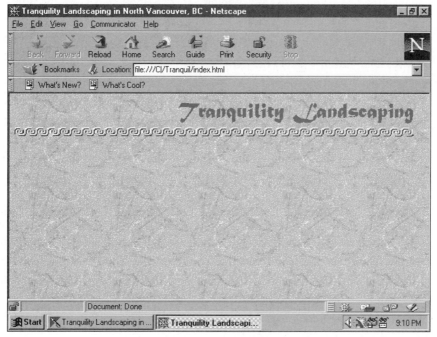

Clues to Use

Obtaining Image Files

Hundreds of sites on the World Wide Web contain image files that you can save to the folder that contains your Web site. To find image sites, search for "graphics," "clipart," or "computer images" in Excite or Alta Vista. You can also check out the Web sites listed on the Credits and Resources page on the Student Online Companion. Before you use an image you find on a Web site, check to ensure that you can use the image without violating copyrights.

activity:

Create the Table of Contents

You will first save the index.html file four more times so that all five pages in the Web site display the textured background, the name of the company, and the custom horizontal line. You will then enter contact information and create a table of contents on the index.html page, create local links to the other four pages in the Web site, and then copy the contact information and the links to the remaining four pages.

steps:

Hint

If you change the page title in the Page Colors and Properties dialog box, you will need to save the file again before you save it as the next filename.

1. Click the **Save button** 🖫 on the Composition toolbar, click **File** on the menu bar, click **Save As**, type the filename **mainten**, click **Save**, enter **Tranquility Landscaping Maintenance Options** as the page title, click **OK**, then repeat the Save As procedure to create the following three files:

Filename	Page Title
design.htm	Tranquility Landscaping Garden Designs
planting.htm	Tranquility Landscaping Planting Options
person.htm	Tranquility Landscaping Personnel

   Next, you will open the index.html file and enter the contact information and the table of contents.

2. Open the **index.html** file, click below the custom horizontal line, press **[Enter]** twice, press **[Ctrl][E]** to turn on centering, type **Tranquility Landscaping**, press **[Enter]**, type **231 Mountain Hwy., North Vancouver, BC, V7L 2J4, Canada**, press **[Enter]**, type **Call us at: (604) 555-5252**, then press **[Enter]**

3. Enhance the text **Tranquility Landscaping** with the **Heading 4** style and **italics**, then enhance the address and phone number with the **Address** style

4. Click after the phone number, press **[Enter]**, type **You can also e-mail us at:**, press **[Spacebar]** once, click the **Link button** 🖉 on the Composition toolbar, type **tranquil@service.ca**, press **[Tab]**, type **mailto:tranquil@service.ca**, click **OK**, then enhance the line with the **Heading 4** style

   Compare your screen with Figure P1-4. Next, you will create the table of contents.

5. Click after the e-mail address, press **[Enter]** twice, type **Table of Contents**, select it, then apply the **Heading 3** style

Hint

On most keyboards, the I symbol appears as a vertical broken line on the far right key of the second row (to the right of the Backspace key).

6. Click after the text, press **[Enter]**, type **Home**, press **[Spacebar]** once, type the symbol I, press **[Spacebar]**, type **Maintenance**, press **[Spacebar]**, type I, press **[Spacebar]**, type **Garden Designs**, then complete the table of contents entries as shown in Figure P1-5

   Next, you need to establish links between each of the five pages.

7. Select the text **Home**, click 🖉, in the Link to area click **Choose File**, click **index.html**, click **Open**, click **OK**, select the text **Maintenance**, click 🖉, click **Choose File**, click **mainten.htm**, click **Open**, click **OK**, repeat this procedure to create links to the **design.htm**, **planting.htm**, and **person.htm** files, then save the **index.html** file

   Now that you have established the links, you will copy the contact information and the table of contents to the other four files in the Web site.

Hint

If you need to center the line containing the links, click to the left of the line, then press **[Ctrl][E]**.

8. Select the text from **Tranquility Landscaping** through **Who We Are**, click the **Copy button** 🗐 on the Composition toolbar, open the **mainten.htm** file, click below the custom horizontal line, press **[Enter]** twice, click the **Paste button** 🗐, save and close the **mainten.htm** file, open the **design.htm** file, click below the custom horizontal line, press **[Enter]** twice, click 🗐, save and close the **design.htm** file, then repeat the procedure to paste the information into the **planting.htm** and **person.htm** files

   Next, test the links in Navigator.

9. With the Index page open on your screen, click the **Preview button** 🖼 on the Composition toolbar, click the links to move from page to page, close Navigator, then close any other pages that are open in Composer *except* the Index page

   Next, go on to enter the text required for the Index and Maintenance pages.

FIGURE P1-4: Contact information complete

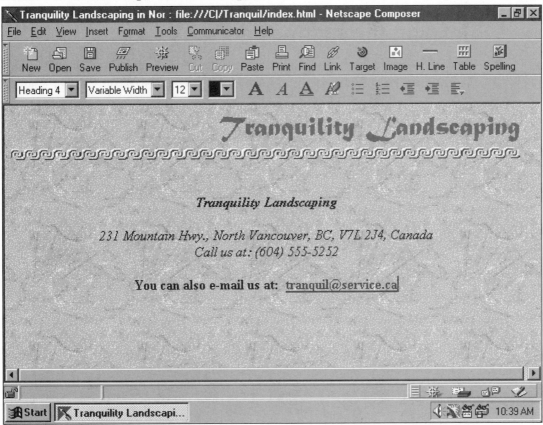

FIGURE P1-5: Table of contents complete

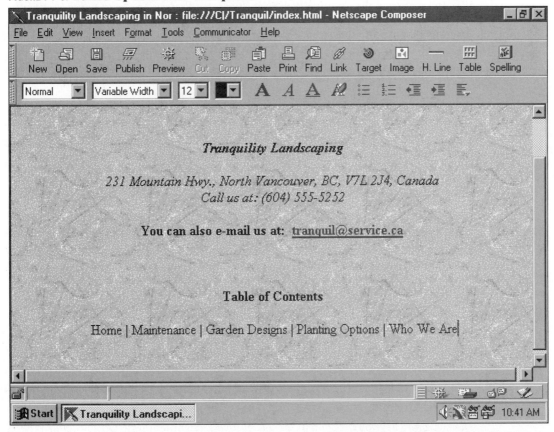

DEVELOPING CONTENT AND DESIGN

activity:

Develop the Index and Maintenance Pages

You need to enter text on the Index page that will inform visitors about Tranquility Landscaping and invite them to explore the various pages. You will then enter the content required for the Maintenance page.

steps:

1. With the Index page open on your screen, click below the custom horizontal line, press **[Enter]** twice, if necessary press **[Ctrl][L]** to return the insertion point to the left margin, then enter and enhance the text as shown in Figure P1-6

Note the directions in Figure P1-6 regarding the required paragraph styles and other formatting. Next, you will insert the custom horizontal line below the text.

2. Press **[Enter]** after the last line of the text you just typed, press **[Enter]**, click the **Image button** on the Composition toolbar, click **Choose File**, click **line1.gif**, click **Open**, click **OK**, right-click the **line**, click **Image Properties**, double-click in the **Height text box**, type **5**, click the **list arrow** next to **pixels**, select **% of window**, double-click in the **Width text box**, type **100**, click the **list arrow** next to **pixels**, select **% of window**, then click **OK**

3. Save the **index.html** file, preview it in Navigator, then close Navigator

Next, you will create links from selected text in the third paragraph.

4. Double-click the word **maintenance** in the third paragraph, click the **Link button** on the Composition toolbar, in the Link to area click **Choose File**, click **mainten.htm**, click **Open**, click **OK**, repeat this procedure to make a link to the file **design.htm** from the word **design** and a link to the file **planting.htm** from the word **planting**, then save the **index.html** file

Next, you will develop the content for the Maintenance page. This content appears in the tranquil.htm file you saved from the Creating Web Sites Illustrated Projects Student Online Companion.

5. Open the **tranquil.htm** file, select the text under the heading "Text for Maintenance Page" (through the word "details"), press **[Ctrl][C]**, open the **mainten.htm** file, click to the right of the custom horizontal line, press **[Enter]** twice, then press **[Ctrl][V]**

Now that you've copied the text, you will format it attractively.

Hint

You may need to left-align the last line of text after applying the Heading 4 style.

6. Select the word **Maintenance**, apply the **Heading 1 style**, select the next three lines of text (to "Here are just a few of our packages:"), apply the **Heading 4 style**, select the three lines that describe the maintenance packages, click the **Bullet List button** on the Formatting toolbar, select the last three lines of text, then apply the **Heading 4 style**

Next, you will insert an animated .GIF file.

7. Click after the colon (:) in the line "Here are just a few of our packages:", click on the Composition toolbar, click **Choose File**, click **star.gif**, click **Open**, click **OK**, click the image so that a border appears around it, move the mouse pointer over the top right corner of the image, then drag down and to the left to reduce its size, as shown in Figure P1-7

8. Reselect the image if necessary, click the **Copy button** on the Composition toolbar, click to the left of **All** in the line "All our packages are available . . .", then click the **Paste button**

9. Save the file, click the **Preview button** on the Composition toolbar, scroll down the page until both stars are visible, compare your screen with Figure P1-7, then close Navigator and close the mainten.htm file

Next, go on to develop the content for the Garden Designs, Planting Options, and Who We Are pages.

FIGURE P1-6: Text and formatting for the Index page

Bulleted list and boldfaced

Heading 4 style

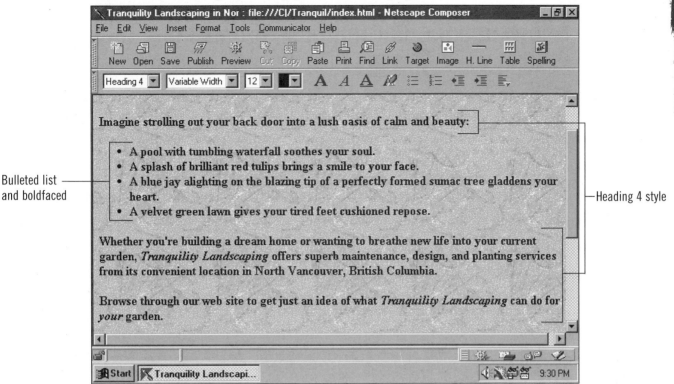

FIGURE P1-7: Text for the Maintenance page complete

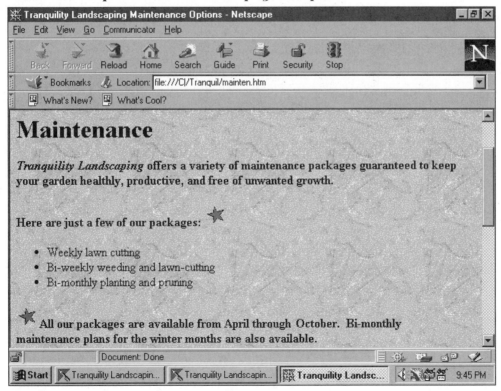

activity:

Develop the Garden Designs, Planting Options, and Who We Are Pages

You need to copy and paste selected text from the tranquil.htm file to each of the three remaining pages in the Web site.

steps:

1. Display the **tranquil.htm** file, select the text under the heading "Text for Design Page", press **[Ctrl][C]**, open the **design.htm** file, click below the custom horizontal line, press **[Enter]** twice, then press **[Ctrl][V]**

2. Select the text **Garden Designs**, apply the **Heading 1 style**, select the remaining text, apply the **Heading 4 style**, compare your screen with Figure P1-8, then save and close the file
Next, you will copy text to the Plantings page.

3. Display the **tranquil.htm** file, select the text under the heading "Text for Planting Page" (through "enhance the beauty of *your* garden"), copy it, open the file **planting.htm**, press **[Enter]** twice after the horizontal line, then press **[Ctrl][V]**

4. Apply the **Heading 1 style** to the text **Planting Options** and the **Heading 4 style** to the paragraph following it, compare your screen with Figure P1-9, then save and close the file

5. Display the **tranquil.htm** file, copy the text under the "Text for Who We Are Page" heading through the end of the document, open the file **person.htm**, press **[Enter]** twice after the horizontal line, then paste the text

6. Enhance the Who We Are page with the formatting shown in Figure P1-10, save the file, click **File** on the menu, click **Page Preview**, compare your document to Figure P1-10, then click **Close**

7. Close the person.htm file and any other open files
Next, you will go on to insert and modify a variety of images to further enhance the Tranquility Landscaping Web site.

FIGURE P1-8: Garden Designs page

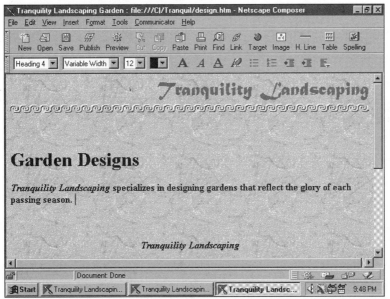

FIGURE P1-9: Planting Options page

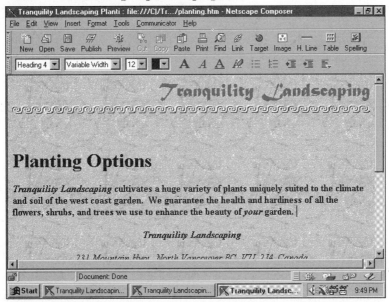

FIGURE P1-10: Who We Are page in Print Preview

Heading 1 ———

Heading 4 ———

——— Heading 3

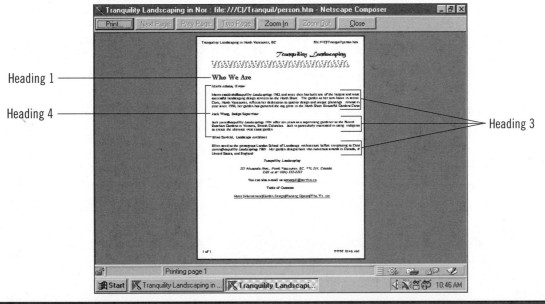

In Project 2, you will insert images that you will designate as links, and then work with the Windows 95 Paint program to add text to an image. Two activities are required to enhance the Tranquility Landscaping Web site with images: **Add Images as Links** and **Modify an Image in Paint**.

activity:

Add Images as Links

Your first step is to save all the images you require for Project 2 in your Tranquil folder so that you can quickly access them as you progress through the activities. You will then insert images as links on the index.html page.

steps:

1. Display the **Creating Web Sites Illustrated Projects Student Online Companion**, right-click the **design.jpg** file, click **Save Link As**, display the **Tranquil folder**, click **Save**, then save the following files to the Tranquil folder: **design.jpg**, **fall.jpg**, **mainten.jpg**, **planting.jpg**, **spring.jpg**, **tulip1.jpg**, **tulip2.jpg**, **who.jpg**, and **winter.bmp**, as shown in Figure P2-1

This process requires some time, but once you have saved all the images, you can use them again when you create new Web sites. Next, you will insert a table consisting of one row and four columns in the index page. This table will contain four images—one in each of the four columns. Each image represents a page in the Web site.

2. Open the **index.html** file in Composer, click to the left of the text, press **[Enter]** twice, press the **[up arrow]** twice, click the **Table button** 🔲 on the Composition toolbar, press **[Tab]**, in the Number of columns text box type **4**, then click **OK**

Next, insert the mainten.jpg image in the first cell in the table.

3. With the cursor in the first cell of the table, click the **Image button** 🖼 on the Composition toolbar, click **Choose File**, open the **Tranquil folder** if necessary, click **mainten.jpg**, click **Open**, then click **OK**

4. Press **[Tab]**, insert the **design.jpg** image, press **[Tab]**, insert the **planting.jpg** image, press **[Tab]**, then insert the **who.jpg** image

5. Click the **mainten.jpg** image, press **[Ctrl][E]** to center it in the cell, increase its size to match the other three images, then click on and center each of the remaining three images

Next, make each image a link to the appropriate page in the Web site.

6. Click the **mainten.jpg** image, click the **Link button** 🔗 on the Composition toolbar, click **Choose File**, click **mainten.htm**, click **Open**, then click **OK**

7. Link the **design.jpg** image to the **design.htm** page, link the **planting.jpg** image to the **planting.htm** page, then link the **who.jpg** image to the **person.htm** page

Next, you will center the table and remove the border around it.

8. Right-click any cell in the table, click **Table Properties**, click the **Table tab** if necessary, click the **Center option button**, click the **Border line width checkbox** to deselect it, then click **OK**

9. Save the file, click the **Preview button** 🔳 on the Composition toolbar, compare your screen with Figure P2-2, check the links, then close Navigator

FIGURE P2-1: Files to save

Save these files

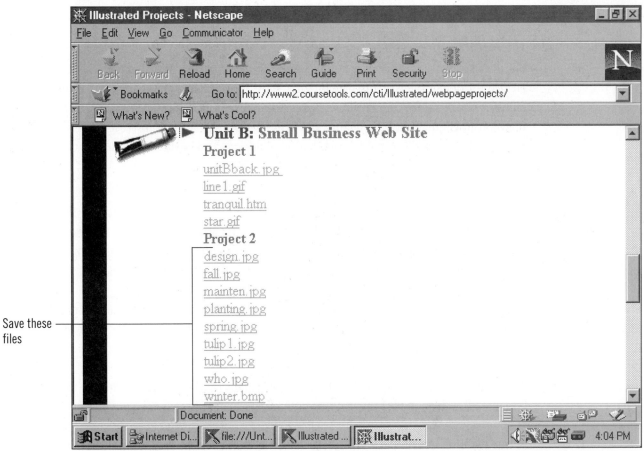

FIGURE P2-2: Index page displayed in Navigator

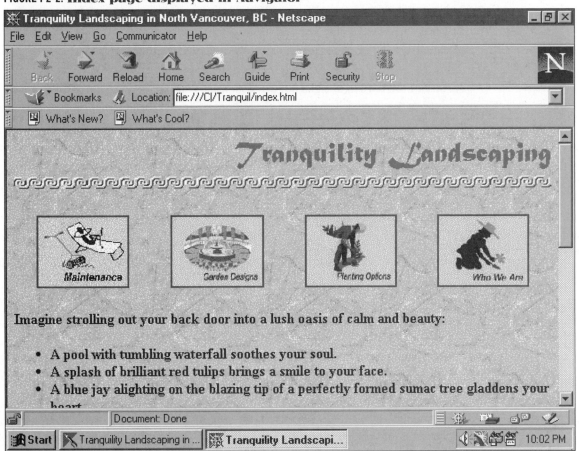

activity:

Modify an Image in Paint

For the Garden Designs page, Tranquility Landscaping wants to display three views of a garden they created for one of their clients. The pictures show the garden in three seasons—winter, spring, and fall. You will first start the Windows Paint program and add the text "Winter" to the winter.bmp image. You will then save the picture as a Windows bitmap file and insert it in the Garden Designs page. Finally, you will insert the spring.jpg and fall.jpg pictures, which have already been modified, in the Garden Designs page.

steps:

1. Open the **design.htm** file, click after the word **season**, press **[Enter]**, click the **Table button** 🔲 on the Composition toolbar, accept the default number of rows and columns, in the Text Alignment area click the **Center option button**, click the **Border line width checkbox** to deselect it, then click **OK**
Next, you will start the Windows Paint program and open the winter.bmp image.

2. Click the **Start button** on the taskbar, point to **Programs**, point to **Accessories**, click **Paint**, when Paint opens click **File** on the menu bar, click **Open**, open the **Tranquil folder**, click **winter.bmp**, then click **Open**

3. Click the **Text tool** 🅰 in the Tool Box, click and drag the mouse to draw a box as shown in Figure P2-3, then modify the settings in the Fonts toolbar to match Figure P2-3

4. Type **WINTER**, double-click **WINTER** to select it, then click the **bright pink color box** as shown in Figure P2-4, or a similar shade that stands out from the background

5. Click anywhere outside the text, click **File** on the menu bar, click **Save**, then exit Paint
Next, you will insert the image into the Garden Designs page.

6. Display the **Garden Designs page** in Composer, click the first cell in the table, click the **Image button** 🖼 on the Composition toolbar, click **Choose File**, click **winter.bmp**, click **Open**, click **OK**, click **OK** to accept the conversion to a .JPG file, then click **OK** to accept **Medium** resolution
You will modify the size of the winter image in a moment. Next, you need to insert the spring.jpg and fall.jpg images.

7. Press **[Tab]** to move to cell 2 in the table, click 🖼, insert the **spring.jpg** image, click below the table, then insert the **fall.jpg** image

Hint

To resize an image, select it and then drag a sizing handle.

8. Click on and center each of the images, then modify their sizes so that they appear similar to Figure P2-5
Next, you will increase the space below the winter and spring images so that they don't "crowd" the fall image.

9. Right-click the **winter** image, click **Table Properties**, click the **Table tab** if necessary, double-click the **Cell padding text box**, type **20**, save the file, preview it in Navigator, then close Navigator and close the design.htm file
Next, go on to Project 3, where you will insert alternate text and low resolution images to appear on browsers that do not support high-resolution images, and then learn how to insert a counter on the Index page.

Select the Arial font

Text tool

Position the mouse
pointer here to draw
the box

Change the font size
to 36

Select bold and italic

FIGURE P2-3: Text box drawn in Paint

FIGURE P2-4: Color selected in Paint

Bright pink

FIGURE P2-5: Garden Designs page in Print Preview

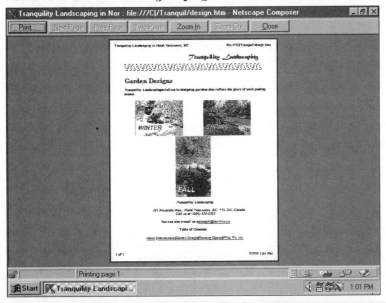

PROJECT 3

DISPLAYING ALTERNATE TEXT AND INSERTING A COUNTER

In Project 3, you will insert an image on the Planting page that is preceded by a low-resolution image and alternate text, to serve users whose Web browsers do not support high-resolution images and who might have slow modems. You will also learn how to insert a counter on your home page that will record the number of visitors to the site. Two activities are required to complete Project 3: Insert Alternate Text and Images and Insert a Counter.

activity:

Insert Alternate Text and Images

Users who view the Tranquility Landscaping Web site with certain browsers may not be able to view images. To ensure that users viewing the Planting page gain some additional information about the company's high-quality products, you will insert an image that is replaced with alternate text if a browser cannot view images. This text will also appear in newer browsers when the user points the mouse at the image. In addition, you will insert an alternate, low- resolution image so that users with slow modem connections can see some kind of an image as they wait for the "real" one to load.

steps:

1. Open the **planting.htm** file, click after the word **garden** in the last line of the first paragraph, then press [**Enter**] twice

2. Click the **Image button** on the Composition toolbar, click **Choose File**, click **tulip1.jpg**, then click **Open**

   Next, you will specify the alternate text you would like to display should a user be viewing the site with a browser that does not support images.

3. Click **Alt. Text/Low Res.**, then type **Each fall Tranquility Landscaping will plant only the finest bulbs from Holland**

4. Press [**Tab**], click **Choose File**, then in the list of files click **tulip2.jpg**

   The Alternate Image Properties dialog box appears, as shown in Figure P3-1.

5. Click **OK**, then click **OK**

6. Press [**Ctrl**][**E**] to center the image, then increase its size so that it appears as shown in Figure P3-2

7. Save the file, then click the **Preview button** on the Composition toolbar

8. Move the mouse pointer over the image to display the alternate text, as shown in Figure P3-3

9. Close Navigator, then close the Planting Options page

   Next, go on to learn how to insert a counter on the index page and then view all the pages in the Web site.

Clues to Use

Accommodating Older Web Browsers

When you create a Web site, you need to think about how the images will appear on other browsers. If possible, try to preview your site on a variety of browsers and screens and then make the required adjustments to your pages.

FIGURE P3-1: Alternate Image Properties dialog box

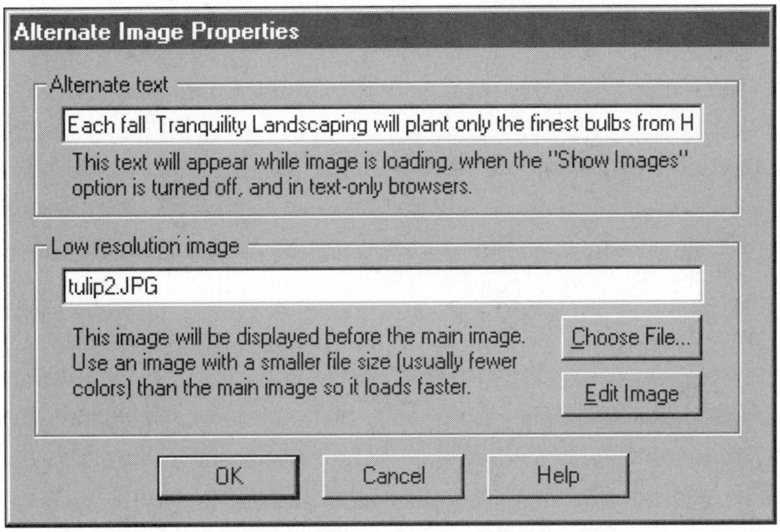

Alternate Image Properties

Alternate text

Each fall Tranquility Landscaping will plant only the finest bulbs from H

This text will appear while image is loading, when the "Show Images" option is turned off, and in text-only browsers.

Low resolution image

tulip2.JPG

This image will be displayed before the main image. Use an image with a smaller file size (usually fewer colors) than the main image so it loads faster.

Choose File...

Edit Image

OK   Cancel   Help

FIGURE P3-2: Image resized

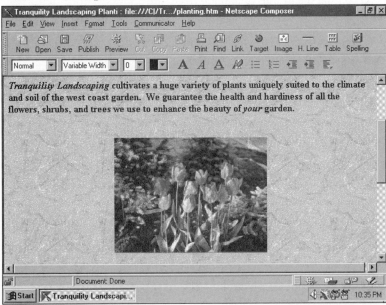

FIGURE P3-3: Planting Options page displayed in Navigator

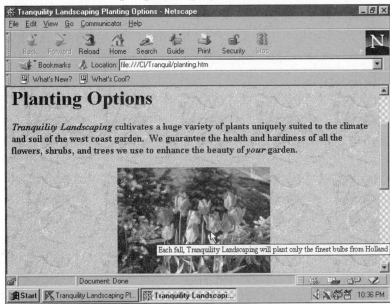

DISPLAYING ALTERNATE TEXT AND INSERTING A COUNTER

activity:

Insert a Counter

A counter records the number of **hits**, or visits, to your Web site. A hit is recorded when a user accesses your site or clicks the Reload button. The counter you insert on your Web site is controlled by the server that carries your Web site on the World Wide Web. You can insert a counter only on a Web site that is connected to an Internet Service Provider (ISP). Therefore, in this activity you will insert into the Tranquility Landscaping Web site a "dummy" counter that is not connected to a server.

steps:

1. Open the **index.html** file, scroll to the bottom of the page, click after the text **Who We Are**, press **[Enter]** twice, click the **Link button** 🔗 on the Composition toolbar, click **Remove Link**, then click **OK**

   This action removes link formatting from the text you are about to type.

2. Type **You are visitor No.**, then press **[Spacebar]** twice

   Next, you need to insert an HTML code that will tell the ISP to insert a counter.

3. Click **Insert** on the menu bar, then click **HTML tag**

4. Type **<IMG SRC="/cgi-bin/counter/member">** as shown in Figure P3-4, then click **Verify**

   If the code was entered correctly, Netscape does not return a message.

5. Click **OK**, press **[Spacebar]**, then type **to visit this site**

   The last line of the index.html page appears, as shown in Figure P3-5. Next, you will view the Index page in Print Preview.

6. Save the **index.html** file, click **File** on the menu bar, click **Page Setup**, click the **Black Text check box** to select it, click **OK**, click **File**, then click **Print Preview**

   A picture symbol represents the HTML tag you inserted at the bottom of the page. If this HTML tag were "active," a counter symbol similar to the counter illustrated in Figure P3-6 would appear. Next, you will print just the first page of the index.html file.

7. Click **Print**, print one copy of page 1, then save and close the **index.html** page

   The text referring to the counter will not appear on the printed page. This text appears only if you choose to print all the pages.

8. Open, preview, and print the remaining four pages in the Web site, then close each page and exit Netscape Communicator

Hint

If you receive an error message, check your typing to ensure that the text appears exactly as shown in Figure P3-1.

Hint

Before you print the Maintenance page, remove the two animated star images or they will appear alone on the printed page.

Clues to Use

Inserting a Counter for a Live Web Site

When you are connected to an ISP, you merely substitute information provided by your ISP in the required HTML code. The HTML tag you entered in this activity is not valid because the site is not connected to a server. To activate a tag for a Web site that is connected to a server, you would contact your ISP, request instructions regarding the installation of a counter, and replace the word "member" in the HTML tag with the identification you use to access your ISP account. For example, if your identification is gsmith, the HTML code would appear as <IMG SRC="/cgi-bin/counter/gsmith">. In most cases, your ISP will instruct you to initialize your counter by opening an internet address (called a URL) associated with the server and then following the directions on the screen. The ISP would then instruct you to enter an HTML tag similar to the HTML tag you just inserted in the index.html page for the Tranquility Landscaping site. The counter you inserted would then appear when you display the page in Print Preview. You can test the counter by clicking the Reload button to increase the numbers displayed on the counter. Figure P3-6 shows an actual counter on a "live" Web site.

FIGURE P3-4: HTML Tag dialog box

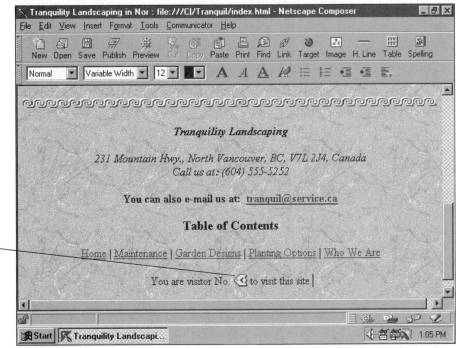

FIGURE P3-5: Reference to counter on the Index page

HTML tag ──────

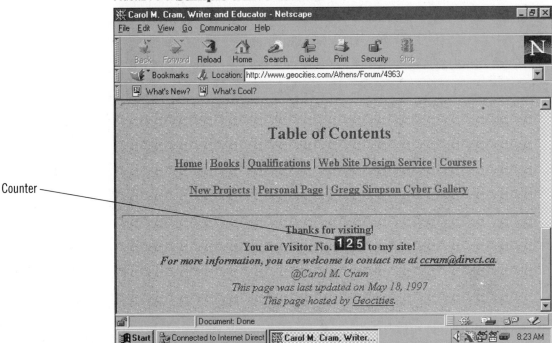

FIGURE P3-6: Sample active counter

Counter ──────

Independent Challenges

INDEPENDENT CHALLENGE 1

Create a Web site to advertise the products and services sold by a small business of your choice. The goal of your small business Web site is to inform the world about your products and services in order to generate interest in your business and, perhaps, increase sales. Follow the steps provided to organize your thoughts and create a Web site consisting of four or five pages.

1. Fill in the box below with the name of your business and a description of its products and/or services. For example, you could call your company Gourmet Catering and describe it as a home-based operation that provides catering services for weddings, corporate parties, and special events.

> **Company Name:**
> **Description:**

2. Use the chart below to create a storyboard for your Web site. Include at least four pages in addition to the home page.

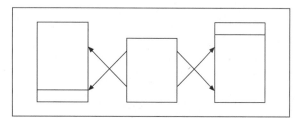

3. Determine the purpose of each page in your Web site and assign filenames. Use the table below to organize your site.

Page Content	Filename
Introduce the business and provide links to the other pages in the Web site.	index.html

4. Create a folder called "My Small Business Site." You will save all the files associated with your small business Web site to this folder.
5. Display Composer and create only those elements that you wish to appear on every page of the Web site. You should select an appropriate background and background colors, include a heading to appear at the top of each page, and include contact information to appear at the bottom of each page. Remember to include an e-mail address (type mailto:[e-mail address] in the Make Link dialog box.) To find an interesting background, search the World Wide Web for Web sites that supply graphics for Web pages. Alternatively, check out the sites listed under Resources on the Creating Web Sites Illustrated Projects Student Online Companion.
6. Once you are satisfied with the overall design of your Web site, save each page with the filenames you have allocated. Keep the filenames short and use all lowercase letters.
7. Open the index.html file and create a table of contents for your Web site. Include all the pages in the site and then make the required links.
8. Copy the table of contents and links to each page in your Web site.
9. Enter text for each of the pages in your Web site.
10. Frequently preview the pages in Navigator and check all your links.

INDEPENDENT CHALLENGE 2

Enhance your Web site with a variety of pictures. You can obtain pictures by scanning your own photographs or by saving pictures you find on the World Wide Web. Arrange the pictures on your Web site according to the following guidelines:

1. Display two or more pictures side by side on one of the pages in your Web. To display pictures side by side, you need to insert a table form and then, if you wish, remove the border (enter 0 for the Border line width in the New Table Properties dialog box).
2. Include alternate text for at least one of the pictures in your Web site.
3. Modify at least one picture in a graphics program such as Microsoft Paint. If possible, use a more sophisticated program such as CorelDraw or download shareware paint programs from the World Wide Web. Check the Resources links on the Creating Web Sites Student Online Companion for software sites. Make sure you ask your instructor or technical support person if you are permitted to download software to your college network system or your own disk.
4. Make at least one picture a link to another page in your Web site.
5. Save all the pages and preview each page in Navigator.

INDEPENDENT CHALLENGE 3

If you are able to publish your Web site on an ISP, follow the instructions provided below to insert a counter. If you are not able to publish your Web site, skip to Step 6 and simply print a copy of each page.

1. Follow the procedures supplied by your instructor to publish your Web site on your ISP.
2. Display the server's World Wide Web site and follow links to find information about inserting a counter.
3. As instructed by your ISP, initialize the counter.
4. Insert the appropriate HTML tag at the bottom of the index.html page. To minimize errors, copy the HTML tag suggested by the ISP, and then paste it in the HTML Tag dialog box. You will need to include your login name in the HTML Tag where indicated in the instructions provided by the ISP.
5. Preview the index.html page in Navigator, and then click the Reload button to ensure that the counter works. If the counter does not display, return to the ISP Web site and repeat the steps provided.
6. Print a copy of the pages in your Web site. To print a page, click File on the menu bar, click Page Setup, make sure the Black Text check box is selected, click OK, then click the Print this Page button. Note that you will need to print each page separately.
7. Disconnect from the Internet and exit Netscape Communicator.

INDEPENDENT CHALLENGE 4

You've been asked to design and create a Web site for a small, home-based business called The Learning Place, which sells children's educational toys to local customers and by mail order. The owner of the business, Sharon Wong, plans to launch an online store in the future, but for now she just wants to establish a presence on the World Wide Web with a four-page site that introduces her products and provides contact information. Illustrated below is an outline for The Learning Place Web site:

Page Content	Filename
Introduction to The Learning Place	
Picture	
Links to Preschool Toys, Grades 1 to 3 Toys, Grades 4 to 7 Toys	index.html
Preschool Toys	presch.htm
Grades 1 to 3 Toys	gr1_3.htm
Grades 4 to 7 Toys	gr4_7.htm

Follow the steps provided to complete the Web site for The Learning Place.

1. Create a folder called "Learning."
2. Display the Creating Web Sites Illustrated Projects Student Online Companion, then copy the files listed under Independent Challenge 4 for Unit B to the Learning folder. The filenames are ic4b.gif, bubble.gif, child1.jpg, child2.jpg, and child3.jpg.
3. Refer to the illustration of the four completed pages of The Learning Place Web site in Figure IC-1.
4. Open a blank page in Composer, select the graphics file ic4b.gif as the page background and create the heading as shown in Figure IC-1. Note that the horizontal line is 10 pixels in width with the 3-D shading removed.
5. Save the page as index.html, and enter "The Learning Place" as the page title.
6. Save the page again as presch.htm, gr1_3.htm, and gr4_7.htm.
7. Display the index.html page, then enter the contact information and create the table of contents as shown in Figure IC-1 (you'll insert the graphics later in this project). Determine which paragraph styles you want to use.
8. Create the required links for the table of contents, then copy the contact information and the table of contents to the remaining three pages.
9. Enter and enhance the text required for each of the four pages in the Web site, as shown in Figure IC-1. Decide which heading styles to use.
10. Display the index.html page, click below the line, insert the bubble.gif image, then adjust its size, as shown in Figure IC-1.
11. Click to the right of the picture, create a table consisting of one column and three rows, then insert child1.jpg in row 1 of the table, child2.jpg in row 2 of the table, and child3.jpg in row 3 of the table.
12. Modify the table properties so that no border lines are visible.
13. Right-click the bubble.gif image, click Image Properties, click the right wrapped text option, then preview the page to ensure it appears similar to Figure IC-1.
14. Make the three images links to the appropriate pages: child1.jpg to presch.htm; child2.jpg to gr1_3.htm; and child3.jpg to gr4_7.htm.
15. If you want, add images to the remaining three pages in the Web site. You can save images from sites you find on the World Wide Web (just right-click an image and then click Save Image As), you can scan your own images, or you can make new images in a graphics program.
16. Save all the pages, preview them in Navigator, print a copy of each page, then exit Netscape Communicator.

FIGURE IC-1: **The Learning Place Web site**

The Learning Place

Our children are our future!

- *The Learning Place* believes in the power of knowledge and in giving that power to our children.
- A child who learns to love learning gets a head start in life.
- *The Learning Place* will help you give your children the head start they need to lead happy, productive lives.

The Learning Place

1801 Maple Crescent, Bedford, NH 03125

Call us at 1-800-555-8890 or e-mail us at swong@mainstreet.com.

Table of Contents

Home | Preschool Toys | Grades 1 to 3 Toys | Grades 4 to 7 Toys

The Learning Place

Preschool Toys

At *The Learning Place*, preschoolers get the attention they need and deserve! We have hundreds of toys designed by education professionals to attract, amuse, and teach your preschooler. Call us for our new catalog!

The Learning Place

1801 Maple Crescent, Bedford, NH 03125

Call us at 1-800-555-8890 or e-mail us at swong@mainstreet.com.

Table of Contents

Home | Preschool Toys | Grades 1 to 3 Toys | Grades 4 to 7 Toys

The Learning Place

Grades 1 to 3 Toys

As children in Grades 1 to 3 learn to read, they expand their horizons into a whole new world of learning. *The Learning Place* has gathered educational toys from all over the world to inspire young children to improve their reading and math skills, learn about the world around them, importantly, learn to love learning! Call us for our new catalog

The Learning Place

1801 Maple Crescent, Bedford, NH 03125

Call us at 1-800-555-8890 or e-mail us at swong@mains

Table of Contents

Home | Preschool Toys | Grades 1 to 3 Toys | Grades 4 to 7

The Learning Place

Grades 4 to 7 Toys

Children in Grades 4 to 7 need educational toys that stimulate learning and help them to build upon the subjects they learn in school. *The Learning Place* offers a broad selection of games to exercise the mind, build math skills, and and explore geography, history, and science. Call us for our new catalog!

The Learning Place

1801 Maple Crescent, Bedford, NH 03125

Call us at 1-800-555-8890 or e-mail us at swong@mainstreet.com.

Table of Contents

Home | Preschool Toys | Grades 1 to 3 Toys | Grades 4 to 7 Toys

Visual Workshop

Create a folder called "Workshop B," create a Web page for artist Gregg Simpson as shown in Figure VW-1 below, and then save it as "simpson.htm". You will find the background texture (chalk.jpg) and the images (bandol.jpg and forest.jpg) listed under Visual Workshop in Unit B on the Creating Web Sites Illustrated Projects Student Online Companion. Create a remote link to the Gregg Simpson Cyber Gallery at: http://www.maikon.net/wcfma/simpson. Save the page, view it in Navigator, compare it with Figure VW-2 below, print a copy, then close all open files and exit Netscape Communicator.

FIGURE VW-1: Simpson page in Composer

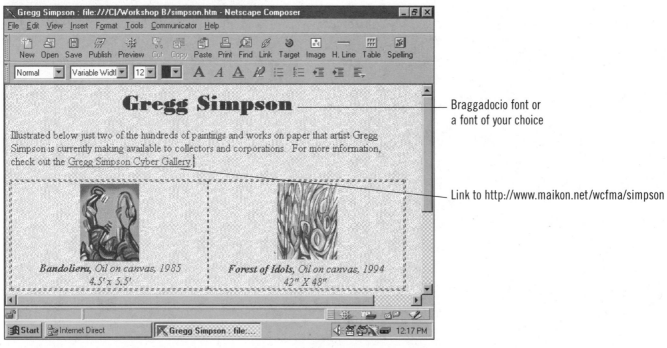

Braggadocio font or a font of your choice

Link to http://www.maikon.net/wcfma/simpson

FIGURE VW-2: Simpson page in Navigator

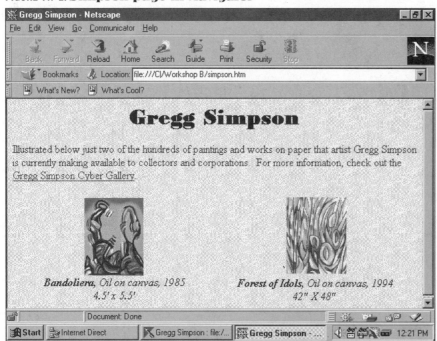

► ## Creating Web Sites Projects

Community Web Site

In This Unit You Will:

► ### Design and Establish the Site

► ### Add Targets and Visual Excitement

► ### Expand the Meta-Information

Local communities harness the power of the World Wide Web by using sites to organize and educate communities around common issues. Local communities can create a clearinghouse of information around a topic, keep constituents updated on fast-breaking news, and inform users about local programs. For example, political groups can promote candidates with text, images, voice, music and video, list up-coming rallies and fund-raisers, keep abreast of current legislation, and disseminate information about their specific causes. To attract users, the site should be engaging, informative, and convenient to use, and should contain meta-information that makes it easy to find using a search engine. ► In this unit, you will learn how to create a community Web site for Recycle to Rescue the Earth, a local community recycling group. Your goal is to make the site engaging, informative, easy to navigate, and easy to find.

PROJECT 1

Community Web Site for Recycling to Rescue the Earth

Before developing the Web site for Recycle to Rescue the Earth, you need a storyboard for the site. Figure O1-1 illustrates the storyboard for Recycle to Rescue the Earth. The main page describes general information about recycling, two pages describe current issues and services offered, and a fourth page will display the results of a contest being held to raise interest in recycling. Three projects are required to complete the Web site.

Project 1

Designing and Establishing the Site

You will begin this project with some research. First you will surf the Web and take a look at existing sites related to recycling, so that you can draw conclusions about what elements you want the Recycle to Rescue the Earth site to contain. Then you will create the site framework by entering generic text and formatting in the first page and using it as a template for the other three pages. You will go on to create specific content for each page. Finally, you will add targets to specific parts of each page, so that readers can easily jump to the information they want.

Project 2

Adding Targets and Visual Excitement

In order to navigate quickly around the home page, you will create links in the headings at the top of the page to targets in the body of the page. From your research on other community Web sites, you know you want to create visual interest in this site, so you will insert animated graphics that illustrate the recycling concepts and help to reinforce connections between related concepts within the site. Figure O1-2 shows an example of the graphics you will use throughout the site.

Project 3

Expanding the Meta-Information

Meta-information is used by search engines and Internet service providers to manage a Web site. In Project 3, you will expand the meta-information about this site, adding keywords and classification content so that search engines will find the site more easily and on more diverse search words. Although meta-information doesn't appear on any pages, you can check the information you insert by checking the HTML code in Netscape Composer.

FIGURE 01-1: Storyboard for the Recycle to Rescue the Earth site

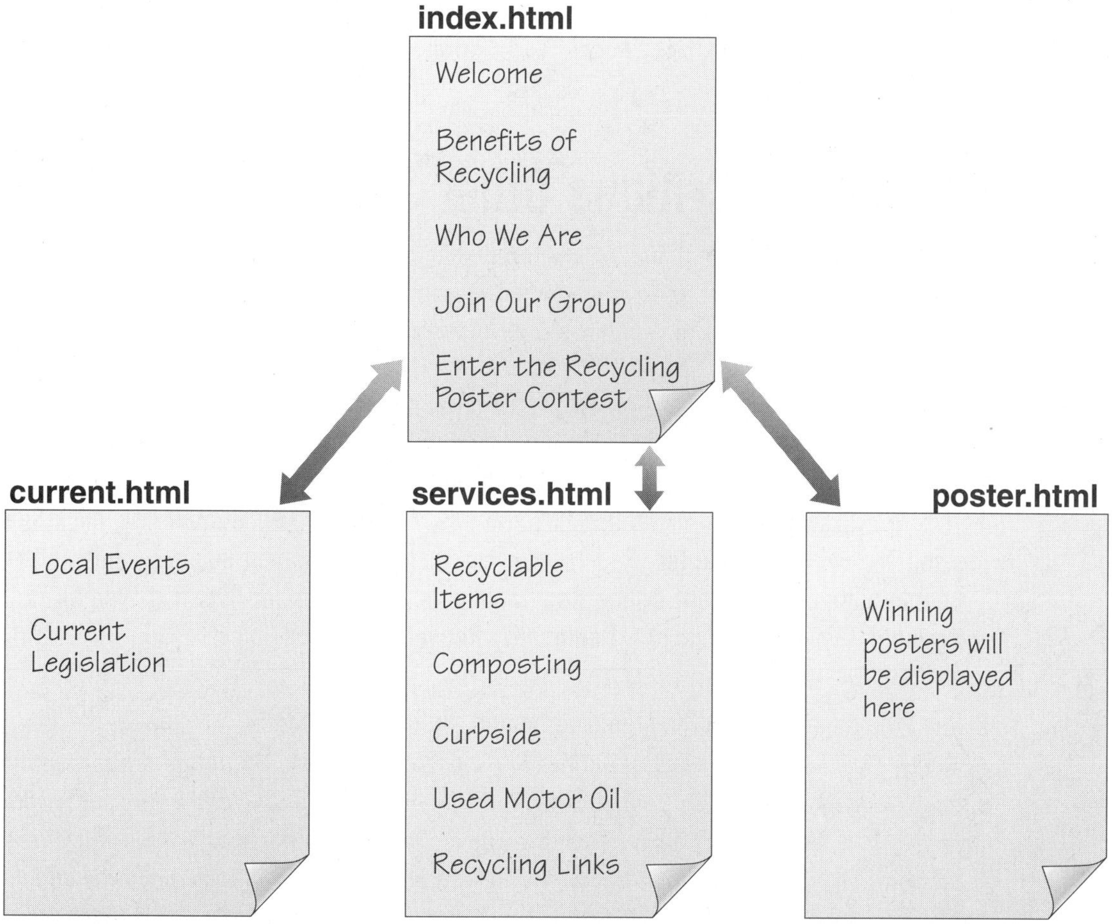

index.html

Welcome

Benefits of Recycling

Who We Are

Join Our Group

Enter the Recycling Poster Contest

current.html

Local Events

Current Legislation

services.html

Recyclable Items

Composting

Curbside

Used Motor Oil

Recycling Links

poster.html

Winning posters will be displayed here

FIGURE 01-2: Graphics on a page

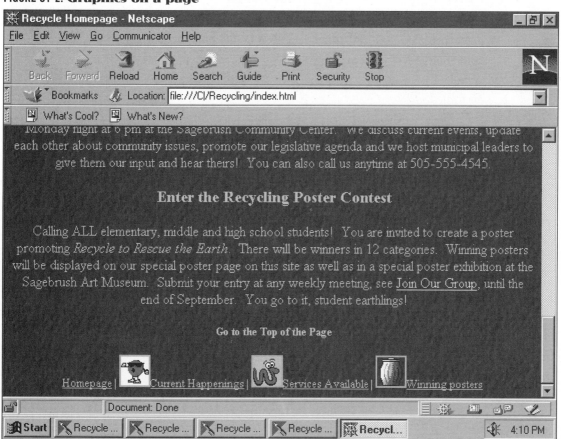

Four activities are required to design and set up the site for Recycle to Rescue the Earth: **Review and Critique Other Sites, Set Up the Pages, Add Content to the Home Page,** and **Add Content to Local Link Pages.**

activity:

Review and Critique Other Sites

When you begin a new Web site, researching what similar groups have already done can give you ideas about what you want to do and what you don't want to do. You will search the Web for similar sites and use your findings to decide what elements your Web site should contain.

steps:

1. Start **Netscape Navigator**, click the **Search button** [Search] on the Navigator toolbar, scroll to and click **WebCrawler**, click in the text box and type **Recycling AND Community,** click **Search**, then scroll to and click **Chapter 4**, or if you are unable to locate the page, press **[Ctrl][O]**, type **course.com**, click **Student Online Companions**, click the link for **Creating Web Sites Illustrated Projects**, then click the link for **Community Recycling I** under Unit C

   The page appears as shown in Figure P1-1.

2. Read the page and note the organization and author of the page

   You can see that there are basic headings in the page, for example, "Building A Community Together" and "Designing Sustainable Communities," but you must scroll through the entire page to know what is on the page. You also can't easily determine who the sponsor of the page is and when it was created. The presentation of the information is visually flat with black text on a white background and no images.

3. Click the **Back button** [Back] on the Navigator toolbar to return to the results of the search page, then scroll to and click **earth wellness festival**, or if you are unable to locate the page, open the **Student Online Companion** and click the link for **Community Recycling II** under Unit C

4. Read the page, scroll to **"earth wellness festival makes a difference"**, notice the last updated date information, then click **The Festival**

   Notice the page displays a section of the page that describes the festival. Next, you'll use Yahoo to search for related sites.

5. Click [Search], scroll to and click **WebCrawler** under More Search Services, click in the text box, type **Wyoming AND Recycling**, click **Search**, scroll to and click **Wyoming Recyling**, then click **Communication Center**, or if you are unable to locate the page, open the **Student Online Companion** and click the link for **Community Recycling III** under Unit C

   The Wyoming Site appears as shown in Figure P1-2.

6. Read the site, click the links, notice the use of graphics, close Navigator, then disconnect from the Internet

   Now that you have reviewed related sites you will write a summary of the issues you want to address.

7. Click the **Start button** on the taskbar, click **Programs**, click **Accessories**, click **Notepad**, then type the elements you want to remember, as shown in Figure P1-3

   You will save this file and all files related to the site in a new folder.

8. Click **File** on the menu bar, click **Save**, in the Save As dialog box create a folder named **Recycling**, press **[Enter]**, double-click the **Recycling folder**, type **Guidelines**, then click **Save**

9. Click **File**, click **Print**, then close Notepad

   Next, you will go on to create the Recycle to Rescue the Earth pages.

FIGURE P1-1: Community Recycling site

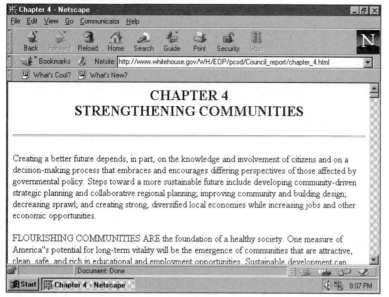

FIGURE P1-2: Wyoming Recycling site

FIGURE P1-3: Guidelines for Recycle to Rescue the Earth site

Click Edit, Word Wrap to wrap lines

Press [Enter] twice to double space

Use the asterisk key (press [Shift][8])

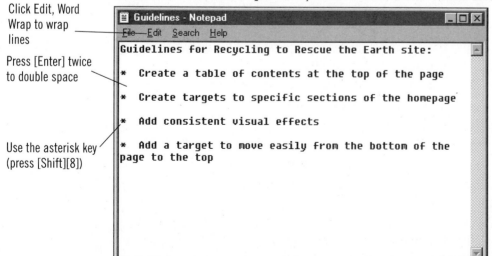

activity:

Set Up the Pages

To create the basic framework of the Web site, you will download the background image you want to use for the site, select the font style and colors, and enter text that will appear on all of the pages in the site.

steps:

1. Connect to the Internet, start Netscape Navigator, open the **Student Online Companion** for this book, right-click **unitCback.gif** under Unit C, click **Save Link As**, save it to the Recycling folder, save the file **world.gif** in the same way, then close Navigator and disconnect from the Internet

   Next, you will insert a vibrant background and logo on the home page.

2. Start Netscape Composer, click **Format** on the menu bar, click **Page Colors and Properties**, click the **General tab** if necessary, type **Recycle Homepage**, click the **Colors and Background tab**, click **Choose File**, open the **Recycling folder**, click **unitCback.gif**, click **Open**, click the **Normal Text color box**, select the **green** in the third row, fifth column, click the **Link Text color box**, select the **yellow** in the third row, fourth column, click the **Followed Link Text color box**, select the **light green** in the first row, fifth column, then click **OK**

3. Click **File** on the menu bar, click **Save**, open the **Recycling folder** if necessary, type **index.html**, click **Save**, type **Recycling to Rescue the Earth**, select the text you just typed, click the **Paragraph Style list arrow**, click **Heading 1**, click the **Font list arrow**, click **Algerian** or a similar style if this one is not available, click **Format**, point to **Align**, click **Center**, click in front of the title, click the **Image button** on the Composition toolbar, under Image location click **Choose File**, click **world.gif**, click **Open**, click **OK,** click after the word **TO**, click **Insert** on the menu bar, then click **New Line Break**

4. Save the page, then click the **Preview button** 🔆 on the Composition toolbar

   Compare your screen with Figure P1-4. Now that you have a background and heading, you can add the names of the local links under the heading.

   Hint

   You can press [Shift][Enter] to insert a new line.

5. Close Navigator, click after the word **Earth**, press [Enter], type **Homepage**, press [Spacebar], type I, press [Spacebar], type **Current Happenings**, press [Spacebar], type I, press [Spacebar], type **Services Available**, press [Spacebar], type I, press [Spacebar], type **Winning Posters**, select the text, click the **Font List arrow**, then click **Variable Width**

   Now you can create the additional pages based on the home page.

6. Click the **Save button** 💾 on the Composition toolbar, click **File**, click **Save As**, name the file **current**, click **Save**, click **Format**, click **Page Colors and Properties**, click the **General tab** if necessary, type **Recycle Current Happenings** in the Title text box, click **OK**, then use the Save As and Page Properties dialog boxes to create the following pages with the following titles:

Filename	Page Title
services.htm	Recycle Services Available
poster.htm	Recycle Posters

7. Display the home page, scroll to the bottom of the page, select **Homepage**, click the **Link button** 🔗 on the Composition toolbar, click **Choose File**, double-click **index.html**, click **OK**, then continue to insert links from the text **Current Happenings** to the file **current.htm**, from the text **Services Available** to the file **services.htm**, and from the text **Winning Posters** to the file **poster.htm**

   Time To
   ✓ **Save**

8. Display the home page in Composer, click the **Preview button** 🔆 on the Composition toolbar, check each link from the home page, compare your screen with P1-5, then close Navigator

   Next, you'll go on to create the contents for the home page.

FIGURE P1-4: Home page with logo

FIGURE P1-5: Preview of the home page with links

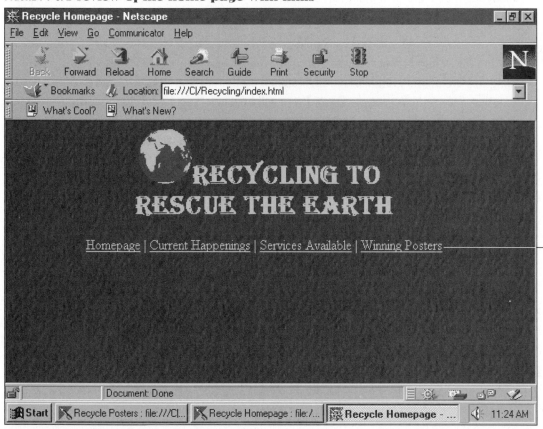

The links are all yellow after each has been followed

activity:

Add Content to the Home Page

Next you will add the text to the home page. You will create the text for targets in this project and then insert the targets in the next project.

steps:

1. Display the home page in Composer if necessary, click after the title, press **[Enter]**, type the text and format it as shown in Figure P1-6, press **[Enter]** twice, then save the page

Next, you'll add the link for receiving e-mail from interested readers.

2. Enter the text as shown in Figure P1-7, click **Insert** on the menu bar, click **New Line Break**, save the page, select the text **Rescue@earthlink.com**, press **[Ctrl][C]**, click the **Link button** on the Composition toolbar, type **mailto:**, press **[Ctr][V]**, then click **OK**

Next, enter the text for the rest of the page.

Hint

When you apply the Heading 3 style, space is inserted before and after the heading.

3. Click after the link, press the **[Enter]**, enter the text below (the text will center-align based on the previous text), format the titles in the **Heading 3 style**, and press **[Enter]** after each heading and paragraph:

Benefits of Recycling
Recycling Feels Good, Saves Natural Resources, Saves Energy, Saves Our Environment, Saves Disposal Capacity and Costs AND RECYCLING IS GOOD BUSINESS!

Join Our Group
Please join hands with your community through *Recycle to Rescue the Earth*. **We meet EVERY Monday night at 6 pm at the Sagebrush Community Center. We discuss current events, update each other about community issues, and promote our legislative agenda, and we host municipal leaders to give them our input and hear theirs! You can also call us anytime at 505-555-4545.**

Enter the Recycling Poster Contest
Calling ALL elementary, middle and high school students!! You are invited to create a poster promoting *Recycle to Rescue the Earth*. **There will be winners in 12 categories. Winning posters will be displayed on our special posters page on this site as well as in a special poster exhibition at the Sagebrush Art Museum. Submit your entry at any weekly meeting, see Join Our Group, until the end of September. You go to it, student earthlings!**

4. Click after the last sentence you just typed, press **[Enter]** twice, type **Go to the Top of the Page**, press **[Shift][Enter]**, select the text you just typed, click the **Paragraph Style list arrow**, select **Heading 5**, then deselect the text

You will create the target to move to the top of the page later in the unit. After you add text, you should check for spelling errors.

5. Click **Tools** on the menu bar, click **Check Spelling**, and then respond to each prompt in the Check Spelling dialog box until the Spelling Check is complete

6. Save the page, preview it in Navigator, then scroll to the bottom of the page

Compare your screen with Figure P1-8. Next, you will go on to add text to the other pages.

FIGURE P1-6: Home page with target titles

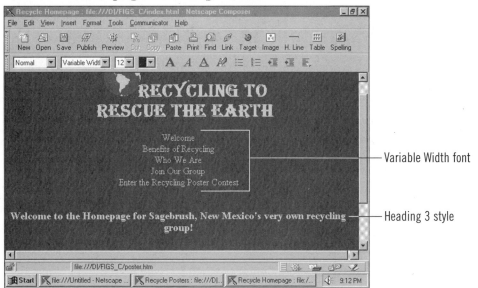

Variable Width font

Heading 3 style

FIGURE P1-7: Who We Are

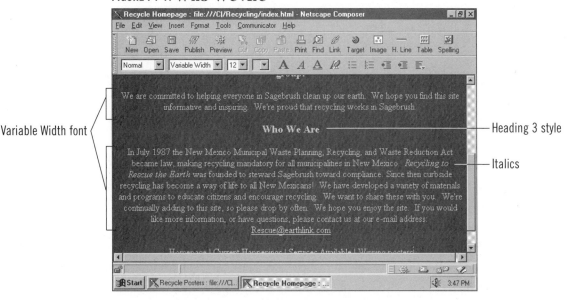

Variable Width font

Heading 3 style

Italics

FIGURE P1-8: Home page with text and targets

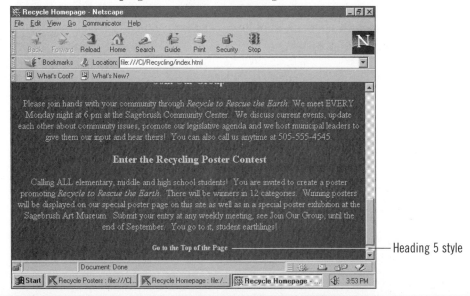

Heading 5 style

activity:

Add Content to Local Link Pages

You are now ready to add text to the three local link pages, providing valuable information to users.

Hint

You can press [Ctrl][K] to remove current styles.

Hint

Select just the page name (and not the paragraph mark after the name) to create the links in the table of contents.

steps:

1. Close the Navigator window, display the Current Happenings page in Composer, click after the title, press **[Enter]** twice, type **Current Happenings**, select the text, click the **Remove All Styles button** on the Formatting toolbar, apply the **Heading 3 style**, click **Format** on the menu bar, point to **Style**, click **Blinking**, click after the text, press **[Enter]**, then enter the text and format it as shown in Figure P1-9

   Next, you will insert horizontal lines to break up the space.

2. Click after the word **Center**, click the **H. Line button** on the Composition toolbar, **right-click** the line, click **Horizontal Line Properties**, in the Dimensions area type **80** in the Width text box, in the Alignment area click the **Right option button**, click **OK**, click after the text **clicking here**, click **H. Line**, click after the word **below:**, click **H. Line**, insert a link for each page of the table of contents at the bottom of the page, then save the page and preview it in Navigator

   Next, you will create the content for services.

3. Close Navigator, display the Services Available page in Composer, click after the heading, press **[Enter]**, type **Services Available**, select the text, press **[Ctrl][K]**, apply the **Heading 3** style, click after the text, press **[Enter]**, then enter the text as shown below and format it as shown in Figure P1-10

   Acceptable Items at the Recycle Center:
   Aluminum Cans, Aluminum Scrap, #1 Plastic, #2, #3, #5, and #7 Plastic, Glass, Drink Boxes/Milk Cartons, Ferrous Metal/Non-Ferrous, Cardboard, Metal, Newspapers, Paper Grocery Bags, Junk Mail, Magazines, Telephone Books, Office Paper, Paperboard (cereal, shoe boxes), Dry Cleaning Bags, and Wood (large quantities evoke a fee).

   Composting
   Free composting workshops to all residents. Workshops last about 2 hours and are held monthly. Call the Home Composting Hotline at 222-POST to request a list of upcoming dates.

   Curbside Recycling
   Recyclable materials accepted at the curb include: Newspaper, Tin, #1 and #2 Plastics, Used Motor Oil (special container required), Glass (clear, brown, and green), Green Waste/Yard Debris, and Aluminum.

4. Click after **Aluminum**, click **Insert** on the menu bar, click **New Line Break**, then insert a link for each page of the table of contents at the bottom of the page

   After you add text, you should check for spelling errors.

5. Click **Tools** on the menu bar, click **Check Spelling**, respond to the prompts in the Check Spelling dialog box, then save the page

   Now you are ready to customize the Poster page. Scanned images of the winning posters will be added to the Poster page after the contest. For now, you will just add the headings for the contest winners.

6. Display the Winning Poster page in Composer, enter the text and insert the links as shown in Figure P1-11, then save the page

   Next, go on to Project 2, where you will create targets and add animated images to this Web site.

FIGURE P1-9: **Text for Current Happenings page**

Heading 3 style

Bold left-align text
(press [Ctrl][R])

Right-align text

Press [Shift][Enter]

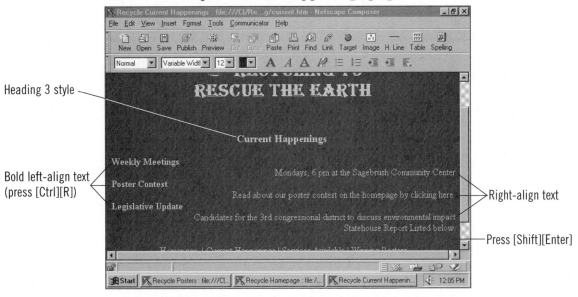

FIGURE P1-10: **Text for Services Available page**

Heading 4 style

Left-align Variable
Width font

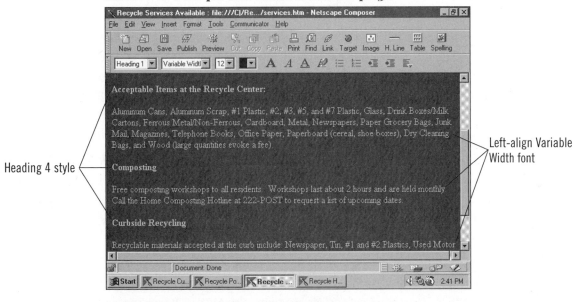

FIGURE P1-11: **Text for Winning Poster page**

Heading 2 style

Heading 5 style

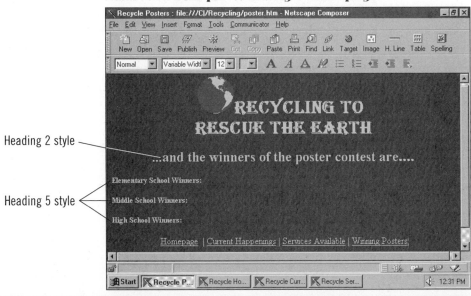

Add Targets and Visual Excitement

Targets and moving graphics are two elements that add sophistication and appeal to a Web site. Targets enable a user to jump to a specific area within a page or to jump to a specific area of a linked page. Moving graphics are visually stimulating. Dancing characters and moving figures lighten the mood and relax the viewer, making it easier to learn. In this project you will: **Insert Targets** and **Insert Animated Images**.

activity:

Insert Targets

You will create targets in the Recycle to Rescue the Earth Web site to move readers from the headings at the top of the page to the topics on the same page. You will also create a targeted link from the currents page to a specific location on the home page.

steps:

1. Display the home page in Composer, select the text **Welcome** in the sentence "Welcome to the Homepage," click the **Target button** on the Composition toolbar, in the Target Properties dialog box click **OK**, select the text **Welcome** in the list at the top of the page, click the **Link button** , under Show targets in: click the **Current page option button** if necessary, under Select a named target in the current page (optional) click **Welcome** as shown in Figure P2-1, then click **OK**
   Now you will check the target and then add a target for the Who We Are information.

2. Click the **Save button** on the Composition toolbar, click the **Preview button** , click **Welcome**, compare your screen with Figure P2-2, close Navigator, scroll to the paragraph beginning "In July 1987" and select **Who We Are**, click , click **OK** in the dialog box, select **Who We Are** in the list at the top of the screen, click , click the target **Who We**, click **OK**, save the page, then verify the target in Navigator
   Now you'll insert targets for the other main topics in the home page.

3. Close the Navigator window, create targets in the home page for the remaining list items at the top of the page to the related paragraph headings: **Benefits of Recycling**, **Join Our Group**, and **Enter the Recycling Poster Contest**
   Next you will link the reference (or anchor) Join Our Group in the poster paragraph to the Join Our Group paragraph.

4. Scroll to the paragraph describing the poster contest, select **Join Our Group**, click , under Show targets in click the **Current page option button**, click the **Join Our** target, then click **OK**

5. Save the page and test all targeted links in Navigator
   Next you will insert a link in the Current Happenings page to poster contest information on the home page.

6. Display the Current Happenings page in Composer, select **clicking here**, click , click **Choose File**, double-click **index.html**, click the **Enter the Recycling Poster** target, click **OK**, then preview the page in Navigator and test the targeted link

7. Scroll to the top of the home page, compare your screen with Figure P2-3, then close the Navigator window
   Next, you will add graphics to the site.

FIGURE P2-1: Link tab of Character Properties dialog box

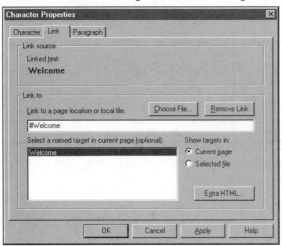

FIGURE P2-2: Who We Are target

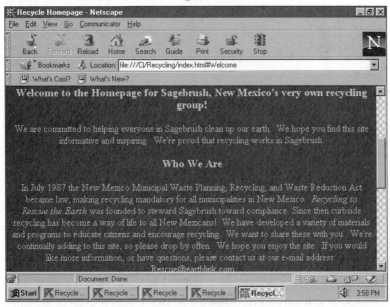

FIGURE P2-3: Home page with targets

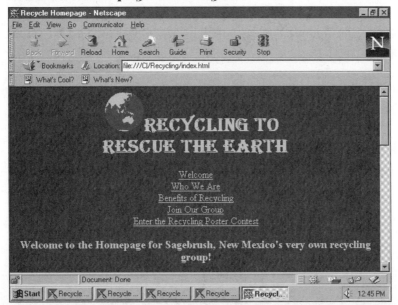

Web Sites

activity:

Insert Animated Images

In this activity you'll insert animated graphics that you copy from the Student Online Companion.

steps:

1. Connect to the Internet, display the **Student Online Companion** for this book, right-click <u>events.gif</u>, click **Save Link As**, select the **Recycling folder**, click **Save,** then save the files **worm.gif**, **gcan.gif**, and **mailbox.gif** in the same way

2. Display the home page in Composer, if necessary, scroll to the bottom of the page, select the last line of text (the table of contents), click the **Font Size list arrow**, select **10**, then click just before the text **Current Happenings** in the table of contents
Next you will insert the animated images in the Table of Contents.

3. Click the **Image button** 🖼 on the Composition toolbar, click **Choose File**, click **events**, click **Open**, in the Text alignment or wrapping around images area, click 🖼 if necessary, click **OK**, then save the page
Compare your screen with Figure P2-4.

4. Display the Current Happenings page in Composer, click in front of **Current**, insert the **events.gif** image, save the page, preview it in Navigator, then close Navigator

5. Display the home page in Composer, scroll to the bottom of the page, click before **Services** in the table of contents, insert the **worm.gif** image, save the page, display the Services page, click in front of **Services** at the top of the page, insert the **worm.gif** image, save the page, preview it in Navigator, then close Navigator

6. Display the home page in Composer, scroll to the bottom of the page, click before **Winning Posters** in the table of contents entry, insert the **gcan.gif** image, display the Winning Posters page, click in front of the text **… and the**, insert the **gcan.gif** image, save the page, preview it in Navigator, then close Navigator

7. Preview the Winning Posters page in Navigator, compare your screen with Figure P2-5, then close Navigator

8. Display the home page in Composer, scroll to and click before **Rescue@earthlink.com**, press **[Enter]** twice, then insert the **mailbox.gif** image

9. Save the page, preview it in Navigator, and compare it with Figure P2-6, then close Navigator
Next, go on to Project 3, where you'll modify the meta-information to make your site easier to find.

FIGURE P2-4: Animated image in the home page

Small target icon— when you move the pointer over the icon the target name appears in the status bar

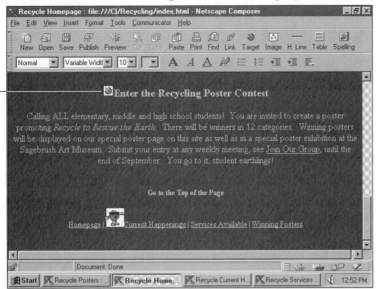

FIGURE P2-5: Three animated images in the home page

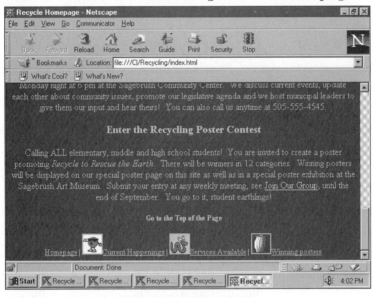

FIGURE P2-6: Mailbox image in the home page

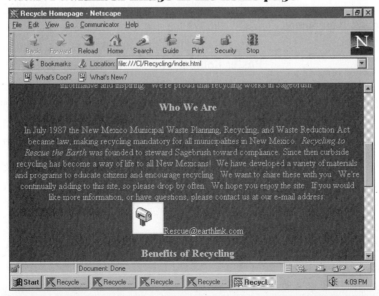

OVERVIEW

Expanding Meta-Information

When you search for information on the Web, you usually type in keywords or select from categories or directories that search engines provide. Because this is such a popular way to find sites, writing the most accurate description, list of keywords and classifications helps ensure that users will find your site. This meta-information doesn't appear in the site itself, but is stored with the site and is used in a variety of ways. In this project, you will **Add Description and Keywords** and **Add Classifications** to the meta-information.

Add Description and Keywords

You want local users (from Sagebrush, New Mexico) to find your site so you will add that to the description. First, you'll write an accurate description for each page and then add characteristic keywords.

steps:

Hint

Be extra careful to use correct spelling in the meta-information. There is no tool for checking spelling for meta-information and a misplaced letter could leave the site lost in cyberspace!

1. Display the home page in Composer, click **Format** on the menu bar, click **Page Colors and Properties,** click the **General tab** if necessary, click in the **Description text box**, then type the following: **An environmental action group, Recycle to Rescue the Earth, based in Sagebrush, New Mexico.**

   The text box doesn't wrap words, so not all of the description is visible. Compare your screen with Figure 3-1. Next, you will add keywords.

2. Click in the **Keywords text box** and type **recycle, New Mexico, recycle contest, environment, green economy, meeting times, benefits of recycling**, click **OK**, compare your screen with Figure 3-2, then save the page

   Next you'll add descriptions and keywords for all the pages.

3. Using the information below, add descriptions and keywords to the files **services.htm, current.htm**, and **poster.htm**; be sure to save each page

Page	Description	Keywords
Services Available	Lists of Recyclable items, Composting Workshops, Description of Curbside Recycling	Recyclable containers, composting, curbside recycling, Newspapers, plastics, aluminum, tin, magazines
Current Happenings	When and Where are local meetings, How to Enter the Recycle Poster Contest, Legislative Update, Environmental Impact Statements	recycling, benefits of recycling, recycling posters, Sagebrush, New Mexico
Winning Posters	Recycling Poster Contest for Students in Sagebrush, NM	recycling posters, promoting recycling, community involvement, art, and recycling

   Next, you will view the HTML to check the meta-information you inserted.

5. Display the home page in Composer, click **View** on the menu bar, click **Page Source**, locate **<META NAME="Description" CONTENT=** near the top of the page, compare your screen with Figure P3-3, then read the entire line

6. Click the **Close button** in the Netscape window, then review the HTML source code for each of the other pages in the same way

   Next, you will go on to add classification names.

FIGURE P3-1: Page Properties dialog box with description of the home page

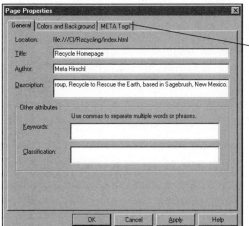

This tab displays optional information that your ISP might want you to include in your document

FIGURE P3-2: Page Properties dialog box with keywords

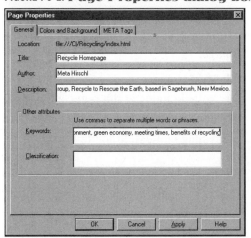

FIGURE P3-3: Source code for the home page

Description content

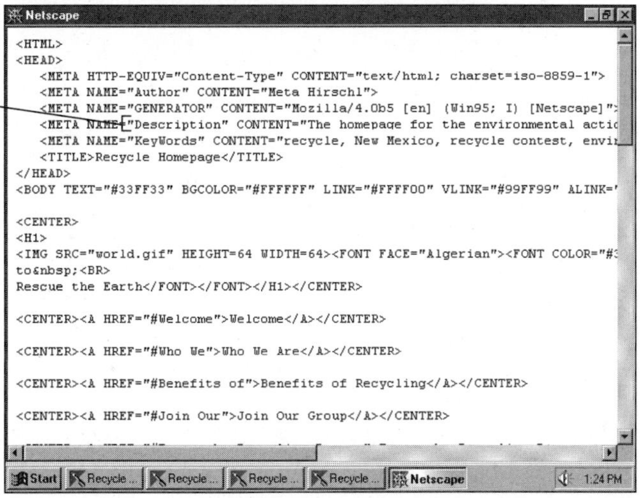

```
<HTML>
<HEAD>
    <META HTTP-EQUIV="Content-Type" CONTENT="text/html; charset=iso-8859-1">
    <META NAME="Author" CONTENT="Meta Hirschl">
    <META NAME="GENERATOR" CONTENT="Mozilla/4.0b5 [en] (Win95; I) [Netscape]">
    <META NAME="Description" CONTENT="The homepage for the environmental actio
    <META NAME="KeyWords" CONTENT="recycle, New Mexico, recycle contest, envir
    <TITLE>Recycle Homepage</TITLE>
</HEAD>
<BODY TEXT="#33FF33" BGCOLOR="#FFFFFF" LINK="#FFFF00" VLINK="#99FF99" ALINK="

<CENTER>
<H1>
<IMG SRC="world.gif" HEIGHT=64 WIDTH=64><FONT FACE="Algerian"><FONT COLOR="#3
to <BR>
Rescue the Earth</FONT></FONT></H1></CENTER>

<CENTER><A HREF="#Welcome">Welcome</A></CENTER>

<CENTER><A HREF="#Who We">Who We Are</A></CENTER>

<CENTER><A HREF="#Benefits of">Benefits of Recycling</A></CENTER>

<CENTER><A HREF="#Join Our">Join Our Group</A></CENTER>
```

Start | Recycle ... | Recycle ... | Recycle ... | Recycle ... | Netscape   1:24 PM

Clues to Use

Keyword Caution

To get their Web site listed at the top of a search list, some Web site writers have been doing a scurrilous trick: They just repeat the same keyword over and over again, thinking that the search engines will then put their site at the top of the search list. And search engines did inflate rankings for sites because of repeated words and phrases for a while. But tricksters beware: Most search engines have caught on to this now, and if they find multiple keywords, they'll just drop the site altogether from the index.

activity:

Add Classifications

Classification names are another method used by searching services to locate documents. Adding accurate classification names can help add to your chances of being found by the right people as they surf the Web.

steps:

1. Display the home page in Composer if necessary, click **Format** on the menu bar, click **Page Colors and Properties**, click the **General tab** if necessary, click in the **Classification text box**, then enter the following: **recycle, environment, green, community, grassroots**

Compare your screen with Figure P3-4. Next, you'll enter classification names for the other pages. To save time, you'll copy and paste information from the page itself.

2. Click **OK**, click the **Save button** on the Composition toolbar, enter the following classifications, and be sure to save each page:

Page	Classifications
Services Available	Acceptable items at the recycle center, composting, curbside recycling
Current Happenings	Weekly meetings, poster contest, legislative update, grassroots education
Winning Posters	Recycling contest, promote recycling, environmental awareness

3. Display the poster page in Composer if necessary, save the page, click **View** on the menu bar, click **Page Source**, then view the classification names you just entered

Compare your screen with Figure P3-5.

4. Preview all pages in Navigator, close Navigator, then close all Composer windows

FIGURE P3-4: Page Properties dialog box with classification names for the home page

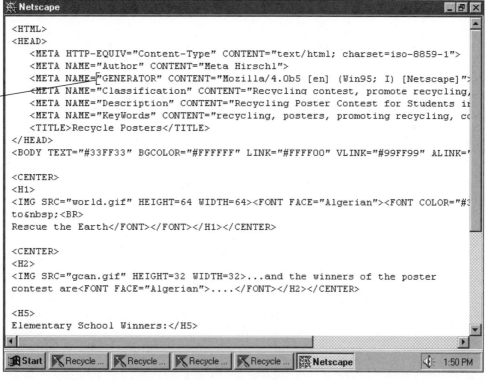

FIGURE P3-5: **HTML source code for classification names**

Classification content

```
<HTML>
<HEAD>
   <META HTTP-EQUIV="Content-Type" CONTENT="text/html; charset=iso-8859-1">
   <META NAME="Author" CONTENT="Meta Hirschl">
   <META NAME="GENERATOR" CONTENT="Mozilla/4.0b5 [en] (Win95; I) [Netscape]">
   <META NAME="Classification" CONTENT="Recycling contest, promote recycling,
   <META NAME="Description" CONTENT="Recycling Poster Contest for Students i
   <META NAME="KeyWords" CONTENT="recycling, posters, promoting recycling, co
   <TITLE>Recycle Posters</TITLE>
</HEAD>
<BODY TEXT="#33FF33" BGCOLOR="#FFFFFF" LINK="#FFFF00" VLINK="#99FF99" ALINK="

<CENTER>
<H1>
<IMG SRC="world.gif" HEIGHT=64 WIDTH=64><FONT FACE="Algerian"><FONT COLOR="#3
to <BR>
Rescue the Earth</FONT></FONT></H1></CENTER>

<CENTER>
<H2>
<IMG SRC="gcan.gif" HEIGHT=32 WIDTH=32>...and the winners of the poster
contest are<FONT FACE="Algerian">....</FONT></H2></CENTER>

<H5>
Elementary School Winners:</H5>
```

Start | Recycle ... | Recycle ... | Recycle ... | Recycle ... | Netscape | 1:50 PM

Clues to Use

Best of the WEB Sites

Another way to increase your visibility is to get your site listed in one of the "Best of the Web" site lists. Examples of these lists are What's Cool, What's Hot, Top 5%, Hot Picks, etc. Getting your site on one of these lists isn't all that hard—usually. You just submit your site to the administrator of the list, the administrator visits it, and if it passes, your site gets listed depending on the criteria of the service. Just go to any of these sites and click on the link to the administrator for more information.

Independent Challenges

INDEPENDENT CHALLENGE 1

Create a community Web site concerning a topic of your choosing. The site could be for a student group you are active with, a neighborhood or political group, or even a local interest group, such as a gardening group, sports club, sewing circle, or book club. Follow the steps provided to organize your thoughts and create a Web site.

1. Determine the purpose of your Web site. Fill in the box below:

The purpose of this site:

The intended audience is:

2. Use the table below to organize your site.

Page Content	Filename
Describe the purpose of the site.	index.html

3. Create a folder with a name that describes the Web site, for example, "Tuscany Golfers," "Sutton Town Sewing Circle," or "Photo Fever." You will save all the files associated with your community Web site to this folder.
4. Connect to the Internet, start Navigator, then use a search engine of your choice to find sites that are similar to yours. Bookmark the sites that you think are especially good and the ones you think exhibit weaknesses. Use at least two search engines to find related sites.
5. Open Notepad and take notes on what elements you want to include in your Web site. Based on your research in Step 4, note elements to include that are visually interesting and comments that will help you avoid those elements that are dull or hard to follow. You may also want to mention sites that you want to include as links to your own site, perhaps on a reference page.
6. Start Netscape Composer and create the background and color for the first page, and then use the File, Save As commands to create the contents for each of the remaining pages. Be sure to include a table of contents on each page. For additional background .gif files, connect to the Internet, go to the Student Online Companion for this book, then click on the backgrounds (backa.gif through backd.gif) listed under Independent Challenges. If you'd like to use one of these backgrounds, save it to the folder for this site. You can also click the Credits and Resources link to find links to sites that offer free backgrounds, lines, and bullets.
7. Select the text colors that complement the background you have chosen.
8. Create the additional pages by using Save As so you copy the background and color schemes to each page. Then add the content to each page.
9. Preview each page in Navigator.

INDEPENDENT CHALLENGE 2

Now that the basic Web site is created, add targets and interesting images to add visual appeal and ease of use to your site.

1. Create links between each page so that the user can not only go back to the home page, but can go to any other page, from any page.
2. Create targets for any link that refers to a specific part of a page. If any page is longer than one screen, create targets within a page, so the user can quickly move to the topic of interest.
3. Insert images to enliven you site. You can find images in a number of ways. You can use the Credits and Resources link on the Student Online Companion for this book. You can use any .gif file from the Student Online companion from any unit, or you can surf the Web for images that you like. Then check to see if the images can be used for free or if there are copyright restrictions. (It's fairly common for images to be available for educational use.)
4. Insert the images that you find in a consistent and logical way.
5. Preview all the pages in Navigator and test all the links.

INDEPENDENT CHALLENGE 3

Now that you have created an attractive, useful community Web site, enhance the meta-information so that users can find it when they query search engines.

1. Write a short but accurate description of each page in the Description text box of the General tab in the Page Properties dialog box.
2. Use an online thesaurus to create a list of keywords for your home page. Connect to the Internet and search for an online thesaurus. If you cannot locate one, display the Student Online Companion, click Online Thesaurus under Independent Challenges under Unit C. Then use words describing your site to find additional keywords for the home page.
3. Continue to develop a list of keywords for each page, using the online thesaurus.
4. Type in the keywords for each page. Then view the HTML using the Page Source command on the View menu.
5. Read each page and enter classifications for each page. Remember to save each page.
6. Preview the site in Navigator.
7. Print a copy of each page of the site. Close all the Netscape Communicator windows.

INDEPENDENT CHALLENGE 4

Create a Web site for a local adult soccer league. The league has a wide variety of teams, including teams of both genders, single genders, beginners, and advanced players. This league has seen phenomenal growth in the last few years and this site is needed to disseminate information to the ever-widening group of participants. The site should include game schedules, scheduled workshops, an advice column, a page of links to national soccer groups, and sites with general soccer information. Use targets and engaging images.

1. Create a home page with headings at the top that are targeted links to the information on the page. Plan what information you want on the home page with targets to it, and what information you want on separate pages with links from the home page. Use the table below to organize the pages, filenames, and content for each page:

Page Contents	Filename
	index.html

2. Create the home page with the background and images of your choice. A few samples are included under Independent Challenge 4 on the Student Online Companion under Unit C. If these don't interest you, use the Credits and Resource link on the Student Online Companion to search for other images.
3. When you are satisfied with the look of the home page, create the other pages based on it. Add the links and targets. Create the content by using your imagination or, maybe, the real schedule of your soccer league.
4. Add animated images to make the site more visually interesting.
5. Insert the meta-information on the META Tags tab in the Page Properties dialog box. You may want to use a thesaurus to help you brainstorm keywords. There are also online thesauruses to help you. To find one, just search for thesaurus on any search engine.
6. Test all pages and links in Navigator. Print a copy of each page, then close all Netscape Communicator windows.

Visual Workshop

You have been chosen to create the Web site for your local dance group, Dancers Delight. Use the figures below as guides as you create the site. Create a folder for all files for this site called "Dancers". Remember to name the home page index.html. Use the Lucinda Handwriting font if you have access to it; if not, choose a font that is similar to the figures. Copy files from the Student Online Companion that are listed under the Visual Workshop under Unit C. The three first links are targets to other parts of the same page. Write the text for these targets and then create them. Create all the local link pages, using your imagination for the text. Be sure to test all the links and targets in Navigator. Save and print each page.

VW-1: Home page for Dancers Delight

VW-2: Events page for Dancers Delight

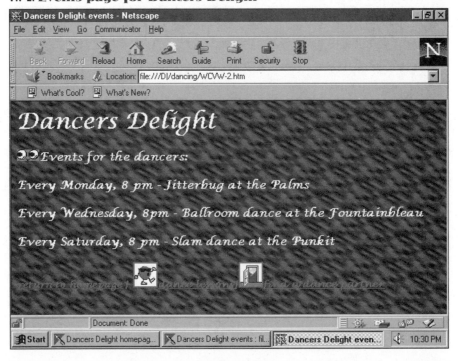

► ## Creating Web Sites
Projects

Information Web Site

In This Unit You Will:

 **PROJECT 1** ► ## Design and Create Frames

 **PROJECT 2** ► ## Find and Insert Links

 **PROJECT 3** ► ## Adapt the Site for Frame-Dead Browsers

The World Wide Web offers such an amazing variety and volume of information that some users say they feel like they are drowning in a sea of sites. You can help users find the information they need by creating a site that lists Web sites related to a particular topic. An **information web site** lists sites that you have already reviewed and checked. By adding short summaries and comments to the list, you further help users to decide which sites are most useful for their needs. To organize your list of Web sites, you can use frames to keep some information, usually a table of contents, in a segregated area that is always visible on the screen. This display method ensures that users can understand the structure of the site from any page. ► In this unit you will design and create an information web site for a health and fitness magazine. You will develop the content for the site, design frames for the site, and then adapt the site so that it supports browsers without frame capabilities.

OVERVIEW

Information Web Site for *Health & Fitness*

As assistant editor of a magazine called *Health & Fitness,* you have been assigned the task of creating an information web site that will attract readers and grow with the magazine. Initially, your goal is to create links to two different fitness activities, running and yoga, as well as links to fitness equipment. Three projects are required to complete the Web site:

Project 1

Designing and Creating Frames

In Project 1, you will create a Web site that consists of five pages and two frames. Frames allow you to display more than one page at a time. You can compare the use of frames to having more than one window open at the same time in the Windows environment. Since navigating a Web site can sometimes be confusing, an excellent use of frames is to keep the table of contents visible as you navigate around the site. And as the site grows, the table of contents will grow. Figure P1-1 displays the framed Health & Fitness Links site.

Project 2

Finding and Inserting Health & Fitness Links

Once you have created the frames and pages, you will surf the Web and evaluate a selection of sites relevant to running and yoga. You will add links to the pages and annotate each link with an evaluative overview, as shown in Figure P1-2. Your goal is to add value for the reader. By reviewing each site, you save readers from visiting sites that don't interest them.

Project 3

Adapting the Site for Frame-Dead Browsers

In Project 3, you will adapt the Web site for browsers that don't support frames. Netscape Navigator 4 supports frames, but older and less robust browsers do not. Since there are plenty of Web surfers who are using either older versions of Netscape or other browsers, creating a mirror site that can be viewed without frame capabilities makes your site available to the largest possible audience.

FIGURE P1-1: Health and Fitness Links Site

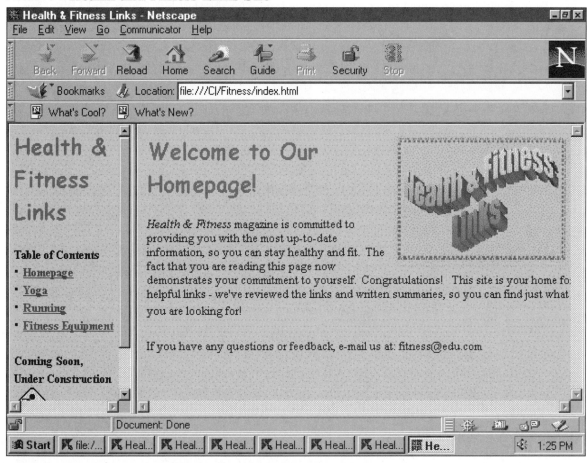

FIGURE P1-2: Annotated link for Fitness Equipment page

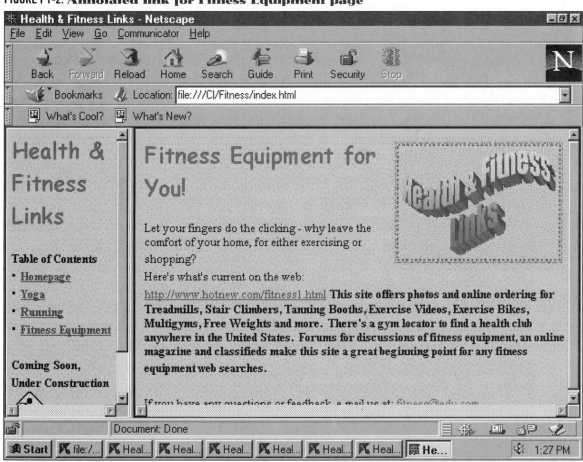

DESIGNING AND CREATING FRAMES

Four activities are required to design and create frames for the Health & Fitness Links Web site: **Set Up the Pages**, **Set Up the TOC Page**, **Create the HTML for the Frames**, and **Target the Frames**.

activity:

Set Up the Pages

As always, your first step is to create a folder where you store all the files for the Web site. Next, you will design the layout of the Web site, and then name and define the main page and the running, yoga and equipment pages.

steps:

1. Create a folder called **Fitness** in the directory where you are storing the files for this book, connect to the Internet, start **Netscape Navigator**, click in the **Location text box** on the Navigator toolbar, type **www.course.com**, press **[Enter]**, scroll down the page that appears, click the **Jump list arrow**, click **Student Online Companions**, click <u>Creating Web Sites Illustrated Projects</u>, right-click <u>unitDback.gif</u> under Unit D, click **Save Link As**, display the **Fitness** folder, then click **Save**

2. Point to <u>logo.gif</u> under Unit D, click the **right mouse button**, click **Save Link As**, display the Fitness folder, click **Save**, save **at_work.gif** in the same way, then close Navigator

Next, you will open Netscape Composer and create a common background and logo.

3. Start Netscape Composer, click **Format** on the menu bar, click **Page Colors and Properties**, click the **General tab**, type **Health & Fitness Main** in the Title text box, click the **Colors and Background tab**, in the Background Image area click **Choose File**, open the **Fitness** folder if necessary, select **unitDback**, click **Open**, in the Page Colors area click the **Use custom colors option button**, click the **Link Text button**, click the **red** in the third row, second column, click the **Active Link Text button**, click the **orange** in the third row, third column, click the **Followed Link Text button**, click the **brown** in the sixth row, third column, click **OK**, then save the page as **main**

Next, you'll insert the logo and create the skeleton of the pages for the Web site.

4. Click the **Image button** 🖼 on the Composition toolbar, click **Choose File**, click **logo**, click **Open**, click ▦ in the Text alignment or wrapping around images area, then click **OK**

Next, you will format the text attractively and then create an e-mail link on each page.

Time To
√ **Save**

5. Adjust the size of the logo, enter the text shown in Figure P1-3, select **Welcome to Our Homepage!**, click the **Paragraph Style list arrow**, click **Heading 2**, click the **Font list arrow**, click **Comic Sans MS**, click the **Font Color list arrow**, select the **orange** in the third row, second column, select the remaining text, click the **Font Size list arrow**, click **10**, select the text **fitness@edu.com**, click the **Link button** 🔗 on the Composition toolbar, type **mailto:fitness@edu.com**, then click **OK**

6. Save the page as **yoga**, click **Format** on the menu bar, click **Page Colors and Properties**, click the **General tab** if necessary, type **Health & Fitness Yoga** in the Title text box, then click **OK**

7. Select the first line and type **Yoga for You!**, select the next three lines, type **Yoga is an ancient art that combines stretching and strength building with relaxation techniques.** and press **[Enter]**, type **Check out these Yoga sites:** and press **[Enter]**, then save the page

Next, you will create the running page.

8. Save the page as **running**, change the page title to **Health & Fitness Running**, replace the word **Yoga** in the heading with **Running**, replace the next two lines with the text shown in Figure P1-4, click 💾, create **equipment** in the same way, replace the first paragraph with the text **Let your fingers do the clicking - why leave the comfort of your home for either exercising or shopping? Here's what's current on the Web:** and include the e-mail information

9. Preview the page in Navigator, click <u>fitness@edu.com</u> to display the Composition window, then close Navigator

FIGURE P1-3: Main page

Image will appear right-aligned in Navigator

Press [Enter] once because Heading Style adds space

Press [Enter] twice

Heading 2 style

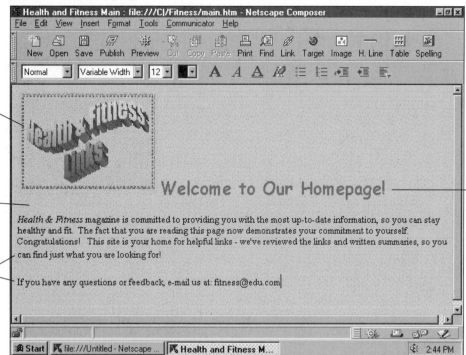

Press [Enter] twice

FIGURE P1-4: Running Page

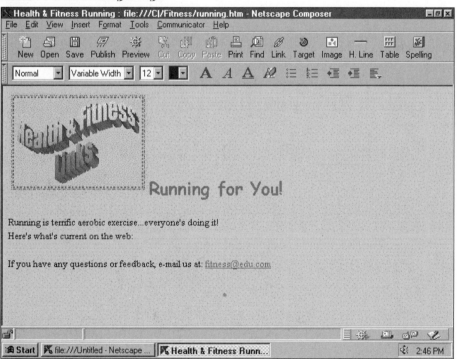

activity:

Set Up the TOC Page

The table of contents (TOC) page will be visible in a frame on the left side of the screen, so that no matter what page users are viewing, the table of contents will always be visible.

steps:

1. Display the **main.htm** page in Composer, click **File** on the menu bar, click **Save As**, type **toc**, click **Save**, click **Format** on the menu bar, click **Page Color and Properties**, click the **General tab** if necessary, type **Health & Fitness TOC** in the title box, click **OK**, select the **logo**, press **[Delete]**, select the title, then type **Health & Fitness Links**

2. Click the **Save button** 🖫 on the Composition toolbar, select all of the text and type **Table of Contents**, select the text and click the **Bold button** **A**, click the **Font Size list arrow**, click **10**, click outside the selection to deselect it, press **[Enter]**, click the **Bullet List button** ☰, click the **Decrease Indent button** ◀☰, then type the list shown in Figure P1-5

3. Select the text **Homepage**, click the **Link button** 🖉 on the Composition toolbar, in the Link to area click **Choose File**, select **main**, click **Open**, then click **OK**

4. Follow the procedure described in Step 3 to insert links for the remaining items in the table of contents list, then save changes to the page

5. Click the **Preview button** 📷 on the Composition toolbar, click <u>Homepage</u>, click the **Back button** 🔙, click <u>Yoga</u>, click 🔙, click <u>Running</u>, click 🔙, click <u>Fitness Equipment</u>, then click 🔙
   The TOC page appears in Navigator as shown in P1-6.

6. Close Navigator

Clues to Use

Frames

In the past, browsers could display only one page at a time. Newer browsers, such as Netscape Navigator 4, allow you to divide your screen into separate frames. Each frame displays its own page, so that you can display more than one page on the screen at a time. One excellent use of frames is to create a frame containing a table of contents, so that users can always see the organization of a site from any page in the site.

FIGURE P1-5: Links in TOC

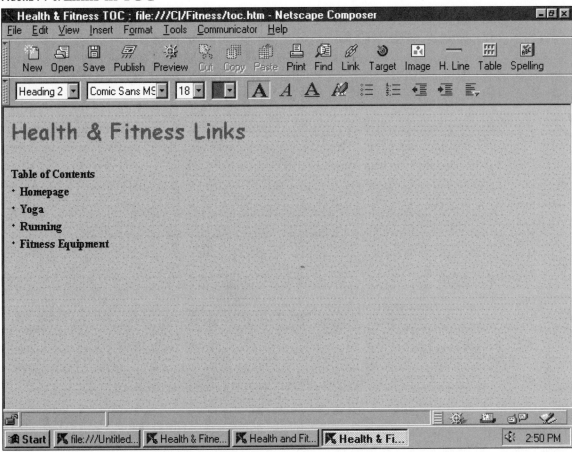

FIGURE P1-6: TOC preview in Navigator

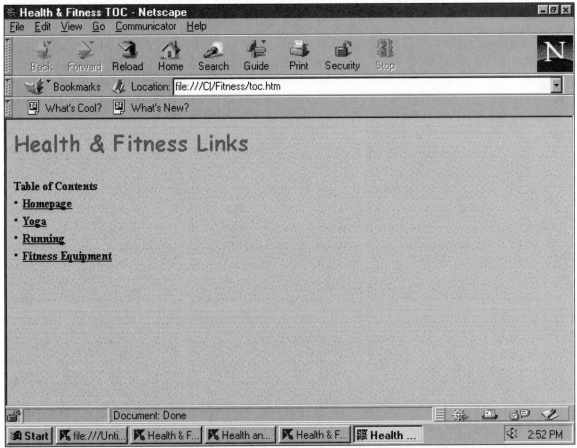

activity:

Create the HTML for the Frames

Netscape Composer does not support the creation of frames with its WYSIWYG (What You See Is What You Get) environment, so you will create the frame page by programming directly in Notepad, a Windows text editor. Even those without programming experience will find that working in the Web page language HTML (Hypertext Markup Language) is simple and straightforward. To program in HTML, you enter HTML **tags** that tell the browser how to display the data. First, use HTML to set up the layout of the screen as shown in Figure P1-7.

steps:

Hint

Tags always occur in pairs, the beginning tag <> and the ending tag </>.

1. Click the **Start button** on the taskbar, click **Programs**, click **Accessories**, then click **Notepad**

First you will save the page that sets up the frames as "index.html," so that the server will know to load it first.

Hint

Add comments to an HTML program by preceding them with <! tags. These tags help you or anyone else to easily understand and remember the purpose of code listings.

2. Click File on the menu bar, click Save, open the Fitness folder, type index.html, click Save, type <html>, press [Enter], type <head>, press [Enter], type <title>, type Health & Fitness Links, type </title>, press [Enter], type </head>, press [Enter] twice, type <!Create two columnwise frames>, press [Enter], type <frameset cols="140,*">, press [Enter] twice, then press [Tab]

Compare your screen with Figure P1-8. The left frame is defined as 140 pixels from the left edge of the screen and then the right frame is what is left of the screen to the right.

3. Click File, click Save, then type in the remaining HTML code as shown below, remembering to press [Tab] as necessary to indent the code:

```
        <!Define left frame>
        <frame name="toc"
        src="toc.htm"
        marginwidth=5
        marginheight=5
        scrolling="yes">
        <!Define right frame>
        <frame name="main"
        src="main.htm"
        marginwidth=10
        marginheight=10
        scrolling="yes">
    </frameset>
    </html>
```

Verify that you have typed the text correctly. Navigator will not correctly interpret any misspellings.

4. Click File, click Save, click File, then click Exit

Next, you will display the framed site.

Hint

Netscape Composer does not support frames. You need to view frames in Navigator.

5. Display Netscape Composer, if necessary, click the Open button 🖫 on the Composition toolbar, click index.html, click OK, then click the Preview button 🔍

The framed site appears, as shown in Figure P1-9. If your screen doesn't match Figure P1-9, return to Notepad, check the tags and text, resave the file, and then preview it again.

FIGURE P1-7: Design for frames

```
Left Frame                  Right Frame

Name=toc                    Name=main
Width=140 pixels            Width=rest of screen
Height=all of screen        Height=all of screen
Content(Source)             Content(Source)=main.htm
    =toc.htm                scrollable
scrollable
```

FIGURE P1-8: HTML to define columns

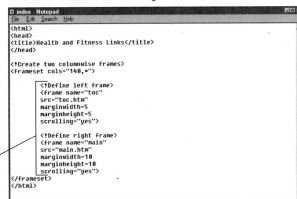

```
index - Notepad
File  Edit  Search  Help
<html>
<head>
<title>Health and Fitness Links</title>
</head>

<!Create two columnwise frames>
<frameset cols="140,*">

        <!Define left frame>
        <frame name="toc"
        src="toc.htm"
        marginwidth=5
        marginheight=5
        scrolling="yes">

        <!Define right frame>
        <frame name="main"
        src="main.htm"
        marginwidth=10
        marginheight=10
        scrolling="yes">
</frameset>
</html>
```

Press [Tab]
to indent

FIGURE P1-9: Framed site

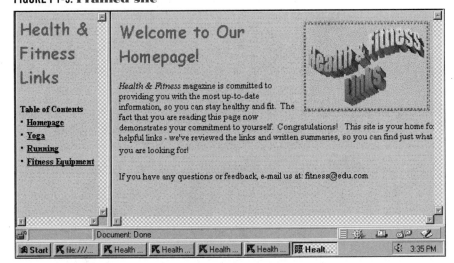

Clues to Use

Frameset Tags

You define the size of the frame with the value list in the Frameset tags. You insert the size of each frame after either frameset cols= (to define columns) or frameset rows=(to define the rows). Table P1-1 details the options for describing row and column size in the value list.

TABLE P1-1: Frameset value lists

VALUE LIST	BROWSER ACTION	EXAMPLE
Pixels	Browser interprets the row or column as a specific size in pixels	\<frameset cols="150, 490"\> refers to the width of the two columns in pixels. The width of the first column is 150 pixels from the left edge of the screen and the width of the second column is 490 pixels. You should avoid using all pixel values, however, because browsers run on all different types of systems and screen sizes. Instead, you should mix pixel values with one of the other value options.
Percent	Browser calculates the size as a percentage of however many pixels are on the reader's screen	\<frameset cols="50%, 50%"\> means the two columns will be split equally.
*	Browser interprets as the rest of the space available on the screen	\<frameset cols="30%,*, 30%"\> means the first and last rows are each 30% of the width and the column between them is the rest of the available screen space.

activity:

Targeting the Frames

Now that you have set up the frames for your information Web site, you need to ensure that the correct page will display each time you click a link in the TOC frame. You can target frames by entering HTML code in the source file, or by inserting the tags in Composer. You'll insert the tags in Composer.

steps:

1. Click <u>**Running**</u> in the table of contents

The Running page is displayed, but it is displayed in the table of contents frame, as shown in Figure P1-10. Once you set up frames, you need to tell the browser where to display the requested page.

2. Close **Navigator**, display **Composer** if necessary, open the **toc.htm** file, then click before the title

Next, you will insert an HTML tag that instructs Navigator where to display the pages.

3. Click **Insert** on the menu bar, click **HTML Tag**, then type **<base target="main">** as shown in Figure P1-11

4. Click **OK**

A tag icon appears in the page. Now, check the source file to make sure the tag is entered correctly.

5. Click the **Save** button 💾 on the Composition toolbar, click **View** on the menu bar, click **Page Source**, then locate the HTML tag **<base target="main">**

Next, you'll test the new target.

6. Click the **Close button**, display **index.html**, click the **Preview button** 🔍, then click <u>**Running**</u>

The Running page appears in the right column, as shown in Figure P1-12.

7. Check each link in the table of contents to verify that the frames and links work correctly, then close all Composer windows

As you can see, you can move easily from page to page using the table of contents! In Project 2, you will add the links and commentary that will make this information Web site a treasured site.

FIGURE P1-10: Running page in the left frame

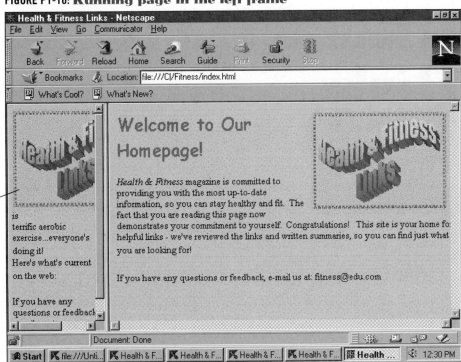

The Running page appears in the left frame before the target is set

FIGURE P1-11: HTML target tag

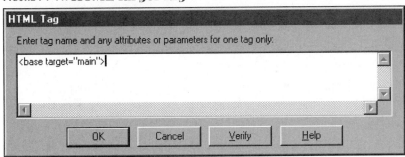

FIGURE P1-12: Running page displayed in the right frame

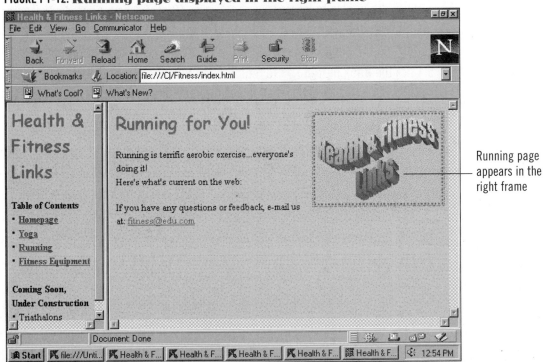

Running page appears in the right frame

OVERVIEW

Finding and Inserting Links

Once you have developed the frames and pages for the Web site, you are ready to add remote links. By also adding useful comments under each link, you encourage readers to keep coming back to the site for more up-to-date and researched information. In this project you will: **Insert Links for the Running Page** and **Insert Additional Links and TOC entries.**

activity:

Insert Links for the Running Page

You can use a number of different search engines and pose the search question in different ways. The key to good searching is having a clear focus. In this activity, you will find links to running sites and add them to the Running page.

steps:

1. Connect to the Internet, click the **Navigator button** 🔘 on the Components bar, click **File** on the menu bar, click **Open Page**, type **yahoo.com**, then press **[Enter]**
   The Yahoo search page appears.

2. Scroll down the page that appears and click **Fitness** under Health, as shown in Figure P2-1
   Since this page appears to have a number of useful links, you will bookmark it so that you can easily return to it.

3. Click **Communicator** on the menu bar, point to **Bookmark**, then click **Add Bookmark**

4. Scroll to and click **Running@**, scroll down the page that appears and click **Running Page, The**, or if you are unable to locate this page, press **[Ctrl][O]**, type **course.com**, press **[Enter]**, display the **Creating Web Sites Illustrated Projects Student Online Companion**, click **running** under **Unit D**, then read the page and explore the links

5. Click the **Back button** 🔘 to return to the Running page, click the **Location text box**, click **Edit** on the menu bar, click **Copy**, display the Running page in Composer, click after the text "Here's what's current on the Web," click **Edit** on the menu bar, then click **Paste**
   Next, you will create a remote link to The Running Page.

6. Select the link, click the **Font Size list arrow**, select **10**, click the **Link button** 🔘 on the Composition toolbar, press **[Ctrl][V]**, click **OK**, click the **Preview button** 🔘, click **Yes** to save changes, then click the link
   The Running Page appears. Next, you'll evaluate the site.

7. Click the **Composer button** 🔘 on the Components bar, click after the link, then type the text, format it in **10 pt**, then bold it as shown in Figure P2-2
   Next, you will read additional running sites and take notes as you go so that you can evaluate them.

8. Search the Web and add two more links for the Running page, including a brief evaluation of each site
   Next, you'll go on to add links to the Yoga and Fitness Equipment pages.

FIGURE P2-1: Fitness on Yahoo search page

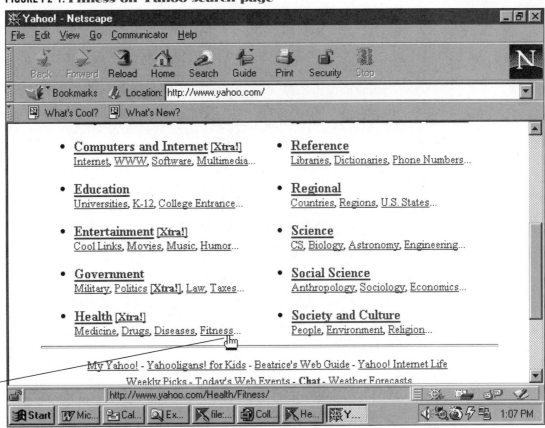

Click here

FIGURE P2-2: One link added to the Running page

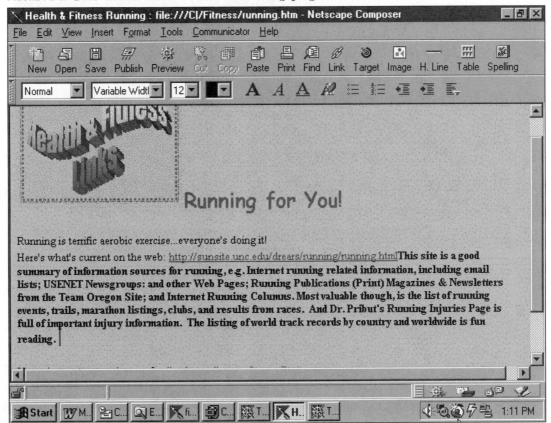

PROJECT 2

activity:

Insert Additional Links and TOC entries

You will now find links to yoga and fitness equipment sites and add them to your Web site. Since each search engine has a different strategy for finding matches, you need to try a variety of search engines. You also want to let users know that the site will be expanding to include more fitness activities, so you will add entries to the table of contents and label them "Under Construction".

Hint

You may need to check the second page of the search results to find the link.

steps:

1. Click the **Navigator button** 🔲 on the Components bar, press **[Ctrl][O]**, click in the text box and type **altavista.com**, press **[Enter]**, click in the **Search text box**, type **Fitness AND Equipment**, press **[Enter]**, then scroll down the page that appears to display <u>Fitness Equipment and Exercise Machines</u>

2. Click the link to display a page similar to the one shown in Figure P2-3, or if you are unable to locate this page, press **[Ctrl][O]**, type **course.com**, press **[Enter]**, display **Creating Web Sites Illustrated Projects Student Online Companion**, then click <u>fitness equipment</u> under **Unit D**
   Next, you will add the link to the fitness equipment page.

3. Click in the **Location text box**, press **[Ctrl][C]**, display the equipment page in Composer, click after the text "Here's what's current on the Web:", press **[Ctrl][V]**, select the link, click the **Font Size list arrow**, click **10**, click the **Link button** 🔲 on the Composition toolbar, press **[Ctrl][V]**, click **OK**, click after the link, type the annotation for the link shown in Figure P2-4, select the text, click the **Remove All Styles button** 🔲, then apply bold to the text and change the font size to **10 pt**

4. Return to Navigator, read the links displayed on the Fitness Equipment site, choose two additional links, add them to the Fitness Equipment page, then add your comments and annotations

5. Display Navigator, press **[Ctrl][O]**, type **excite.com**, press **[Enter]**, click in the **Search text box**, type **Yoga**, press **[Enter]**, review the links displayed, find three links, copy them to the Yoga page, create the links, annotate them, then test each link in Navigator
   Next, you'll add entries to the Table of Contents.

6. Open the **toc.htm** file in Composer, press **[Enter]**, press the **Bullet List button** 🔲 twice, press **[Ctrl][K]**, press **[Enter]**, then type the entries shown in Figure P2-5
   Since these pages aren't yet active, you won't create links for them. Instead, you will insert the "Under Construction" icon you saved from the Student Online Companion.

7. Click after the text "Under Construction", press **[Enter]**, click the **Image button** 🔲 on the Composition toolbar, click **Choose File**, double-click **at_work.gif**, click **Open**, click **OK**, then adjust the size and placement of the icon if necessary, so that it appears as shown in Figure P2-5

8. Save the page, preview it in Navigator, close Navigator, disconnect from the Internet, then return to Composer
   Next, you'll go on to insert HTML that will allow browsers without frames to view your site.

FIGURE P2-3: Fitness Zone page

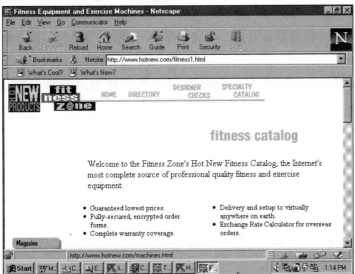

FIGURE P2-4: Fitness Equipment page with link

annotated link

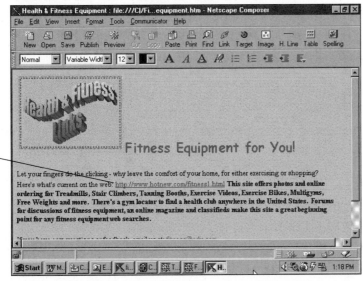

FIGURE P2-5: Table of Contents with image

Icon inserted

Add these entries

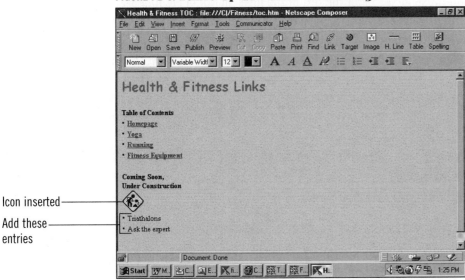

OVERVIEW

Adapting the Site for Frame-Dead Browsers

The recent versions of the two most popular browsers, Netscape Navigator and Internet Explorer, support frames. However, earlier versions of these and other browsers do not display frames. Because you want your site to be available to as many readers as possible, you should add HTML that allows all users to view your site, even if their browsers don't support frames. In this project, you will **Create a Non-Frame Main Page** and **Add the HTML for Non-Frames**.

activity:

Create a Non-Frame Main Page

To create a non-frame main page, you will create a page that contains the same information as the TOC page and the Home page. You will add links to the other pages on the Home page, instead of using the table of contents frame to navigate your site.

steps:

1. Display the main.htm page in Composer, click **File** on the menu bar, click **Save As**, then save the page as **main no frames**

Since the no frames main page will not display a table of contents page, you need to create a table for the links.

2. Click in the blank line above the text "If you have any questions," click the **Table button** in the Composition toolbar, type **3** in the Number of rows text box, type **2** in the Number of columns text box if necessary, click the **Center option button** in the Table Alignment area, click the **Include caption checkbox**, type **80** in the Table width text box, compare your screen with Figure P3-1, then click **OK**

Next, you'll enter the caption and insert the links.

3. Type **Check out these links:**, enter the text of the links shown in Figure P3-2, select the text in the table, click **Format** on the menu bar, click **Align**, then click **Center**

4. Click to the left of the text "Under Construction", then insert the **at_work** image

5. Select the <u>Yoga</u> link, click the **Link button** on the Composition toolbar, click **Choose File**, select **yoga**, click **Open**, click **OK**, then insert links to the Running and Fitness Equipment pages

6. Click the **Preview button** on the Composition toolbar, click **Yes** to save changes, check each link, then close Navigator

Next you'll copy the HTML code for this page.

Hint

Remember to click the File of type list arrow and select All Files (*.*) when you are retrieving .HTM files in Notepad.

7. Start Notepad, click **File** on the menu bar, click **Open**, double-click **main no frames**, select everything after </head> and before </html> as shown in Figures P3-3 and P3-4, then press **[Ctrl][C]**

In the next lesson, you'll paste the no frames HTML to the page than contains the frame code.

FIGURE P3-1: New Table Properties dialog box

FIGURE P3-2: Links added to no frames main page

FIGURE P3-3: HTML code selected – top half of screen

Inserted below
</HEAD> tag

FIGURE P3-4: HTML code selected – bottom half of screen

Inserted before
</HTML> tag

activity:

Add the HTML for Non-Frames

The HTML for the non-frame main page is now on the Clipboard. You will add <no frames> HTML tags in the frame main page for the non-frame code, and then paste the code on the Clipboard between these tags. Then, when a browser without frame capability loads the frame page, it will display the code between the no frames tags. Notepad should still be open on your screen.

steps:

1. Open the **index.html** file, then position the cursor to just below the first <frameset> tag, "<frameset cols="140,*">"
Next, you'll insert a tag for browsers without frame capability.

2. Type **<noframes>**, press **[Enter]** twice, type **</noframes>** as shown in Figure P3-5, position the cursor between the two tags you just typed, then press **[Ctrl][V]**
The HTML code for the main page without frames is inserted in the code, as shown in Figure P3-6.

3. Click **File** on the menu bar, click **Save**, then close Notepad
Since you are using a frames capable browser, you won't be able to test this code with Navigator. However, you can view the no frames page in Composer because it does not support frames.

Hint

If the Index page does not appear, start Notepad and check that the noframes tag pair is correctly placed in the code.

4. Click the **Open button** 🖼 on the Composition toolbar, click **index.html**, then click **Open**
The no frames main page appears in Composer as shown in Figure P3-7. Since the frames index isn't visible, Composer displays the main no frames page.

5. Click the **Preview button** 🖼 on the Composition toolbar
The framed page appears because Navigator supports frames. Next, you'll print copies of the each of the main pages

6. Open the **main no frames**.htm file, click 🖼, check each link, return to the Home page, then click the **Print button** 🖼 on the Navigator toolbar
Next, you will insert links in each page to the other pages, because there isn't a table of contents to move between pages for the main no frames page.

7. Display the running.htm file in Composer, add links to the Home page, Yoga page, and Fitness Equipment page, then add links to the other pages in the Yoga and Fitness Equipment pages

8. Test the links in all the pages in Navigator

9. Close Navigator and all Composer windows
You have successfully created a framed Web site as well as a mirror site that any non-frame browser can display.

FIGURE P3-5: Insert <noframes> tag

New tags

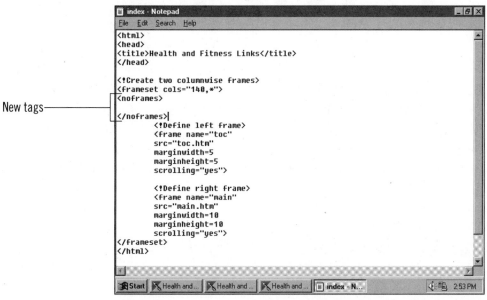

```
<html>
<head>
<title>Health and Fitness Links</title>
</head>

<!Create two columnwise frames>
<frameset cols="140,*">
<noframes>

</noframes>
        <!Define left frame>
        <Frame name="toc"
        src="toc.htm"
        marginwidth=5
        marginheight=5
        scrolling="yes">

        <!Define right frame>
        <frame name="main"
        src="main.htm"
        marginwidth=10
        marginheight=10
        scrolling="yes">
</frameset>
</html>
```

FIGURE P3-6: Code inserted in index.htm

No frames code

Continues below
screen

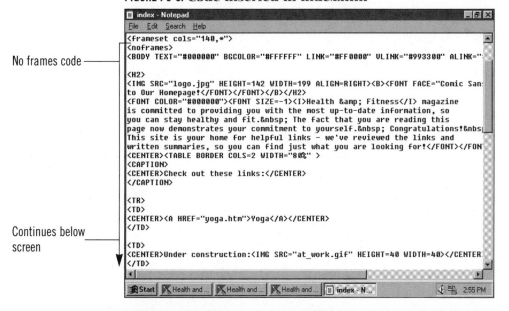

```
<frameset cols="140,*">
<noframes>
<BODY TEXT="#000000" BGCOLOR="#FFFFFF" LINK="#FF0000" VLINK="#993300" ALINK="

<H2>
<IMG SRC="logo.jpg" HEIGHT=142 WIDTH=199 ALIGN=RIGHT><B><FONT FACE="Comic San
to Our Homepage!</FONT></FONT></B></H2>
<FONT COLOR="#000000"><FONT SIZE=-1><I>Health &amp; Fitness</I> magazine
is committed to providing you with the most up-to-date information, so
you can stay healthy and fit.  The fact that you are reading this
page now demonstrates your commitment to yourself.  Congratulations!&nbs
This site is your home for helpful links - we've reviewed the links and
written summaries, so you can find just what you are looking for!</FONT></FON
<CENTER><TABLE BORDER COLS=2 WIDTH="80%" >
<CAPTION>
<CENTER>Check out these links:</CENTER>
</CAPTION>

<TR>
<TD>
<CENTER><A HREF="yoga.htm">Yoga</A></CENTER>
</TD>

<TD>
<CENTER>Under construction:<IMG SRC="at_work.gif" HEIGHT=40 WIDTH=40></CENTER
</TD>
```

FIGURE P3-7: No frames main in Composer

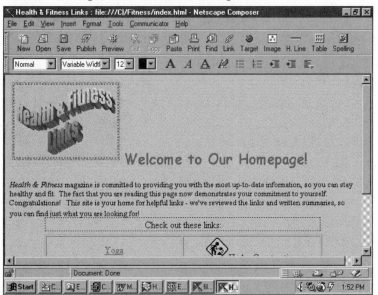

Independent Challenges

INDEPENDENT CHALLENGE 1

Create an information web site concerning a topic of your choice. The goal of the web site could be to provide a summary of links related to a topic such as travelling to the Far East, purchasing books on the Web, viewing video clips, or locating universities offering classes on the Web. The site should contain at least three pages to link to, in addition to the home page. For example, an information web site on travel to the Far East might contain one page on accommodations, one page on places of historical interest, and one page on guided tour programs. Follow the steps provided to organize your thoughts and create a web site.

1. Determine the purpose of your Web site. Use the table below to organize your site.

Contents	Filename
Describe the purpose of the site	main.htm
Page 1:	
Page 2:	
Page 3:	
Under Construction entry:	
Under Construction entry:	

2. Use the table below to define the structure of the frame (index.html):

Left Frame	Right Frame
Name=	Name=
Width=	Width=
Height=	Height=
Contents (Source)=	Contents (Source)=
scrollable=	scrollable=

3. Create a folder with a name that describes the Web site, for example, "Far East," "Groovy Video Clips," or "Buying Books." You will save all the files associated with your personal Web site to this folder.
4. Display Netscape Composer and create the background and color for the first page, and then use the Save As dialog box to create each of the remaining pages. Be sure to include a table of contents page.
5. Create the HTML in Notepad for the framed page. Save this page as index.htm. (*Hint:* You can reuse the HTML you created in this unit by opening the index.htm created in the Fitness folder, clicking File on the menu bar, Save As, and then saving it with a new name. Then edit the HTML with your new variables.) Preview the frame page in Navigator. Test the table of contents links. Notice the page is displayed in the left frame.
6. In Composer, insert an HTML tag in the table of contents page that targets the right frame for display. Preview the site and check that all the links work properly.

INDEPENDENT CHALLENGE 2

Now that you have created the basic information site, surf the World Wide Web and find links that your readers will appreciate.

1. Connect to the Internet and search for pages for your Web site. Read each page and follow links so that you can evaluate the site. Use at least two different search engines in your searches.
2. When you find a site that you want to include in your Web site, click in the Location text box, press [Ctrl][C], display the page in Composer, position the cursor where you want the link, then press [Ctrl][V] to paste the link on your page. Then select the link and use the Link button on the Composition toolbar to create the link.
3. Include a summary of each site you include a link to, and give a short evaluation of it. Be sure to tell the reader why you've included the link on your site.
4. Continue to surf the Web for each of your Web pages. You might want to try search engines you haven't used before, such as HotBot.
5. Add "Under Construction" entries to the table of contents page. Insert the icon "at_work" that you downloaded from the Student Online Companion for this unit.
6. Preview all the pages in Navigator and test all the remote links.

INDEPENDENT CHALLENGE 3

Now that you have a Web site that displays frames, adapt it so that visitors with browsers that don't support frames can view it.

1. Save your Home page under a new name and modify it so that it doesn't use frames. Add all the links that are on the framed table of contents page. Be sure to test the links when you are previewing the page in Navigator.
2. Once you are satisfied with the look of the home page, go to Notepad and open the new no frames home page. Select everything after </head> and before </html>.
3. Open the Index page for your framed Web site, insert the <noframes> </noframes> tags just below the first <frameset> tag. Paste the contents of the Clipboard between the tags.
4. Save the file index.htm, close Notepad, and then view the site without frames in Composer and with the frames in Navigator.
5. Add links to each page to each of the other pages. Preview the site and test all the links.
6. Print a copy of the site both with and without frames. Close all the Netscape Communicator windows.

INDEPENDENT CHALLENGE 4

You have decided to create a Web site for this course that organizes all the links for each unit. Create a Web site with a table of contents in a left frame that lists all the units for this textbook. Each unit then has its own page that lists at least 5 of the links used in that unit. The last 2 units are listed as "Under Construction" and you can fill those pages in as you complete this book.

1. Use the table below to organize the pages and names:

CONTENTS	FILENAME
	main.htm
	aunit.htm
	bunit.htm
	cunit.htm
	dunit.htm
	eunit.htm
	funit.htm

2. Use the table below to define the structure of the frame:

Left Frame	Right Frame
Name=	Name=
Width=	Width=
Height=	Height=
Contents (Source)=	Contents (Source)=
scrollable=	scrollable=

3. Create the page for each of the pages. Add the links for units A through C, create annotations for each link that describe how you used the link for the unit and your impression of it. Then add the links for this unit along with the annotations you have already created.
4. Create the frame page using Notepad, and then preview it in Navigator.
5. Create a Home page that has links instead of a table of contents in a frame. Then modify the HTML of the frame page to include non-frame browsers.
6. Test all pages and links in Navigator. Print a copy of each page, including the table of contents. Then close all Netscape Communicator windows.

Visual Workshop

As you work with Web pages and spend time surfing the World Wide Web, you should be aware of the potential dangers of viruses. To help alert your friends in cyberspace, you create a Web site that pulls together information on viruses and virus detection software. Create a folder called "VirusInfo", and then copy VWlogo and VWback from the Course Technology Student Online Companion under Unit D to your folder. Using the figure below as your guide, create the Web site, and then search the Web for links that cover the topics. Note that there are no scrollable frames in the figure. List at least three links for each page with a brief description of the site. Be sure to include the two top-selling anti-virus software packages, Norton and McAfee, in your page of Virus Fixes.

FIGURE VW-1

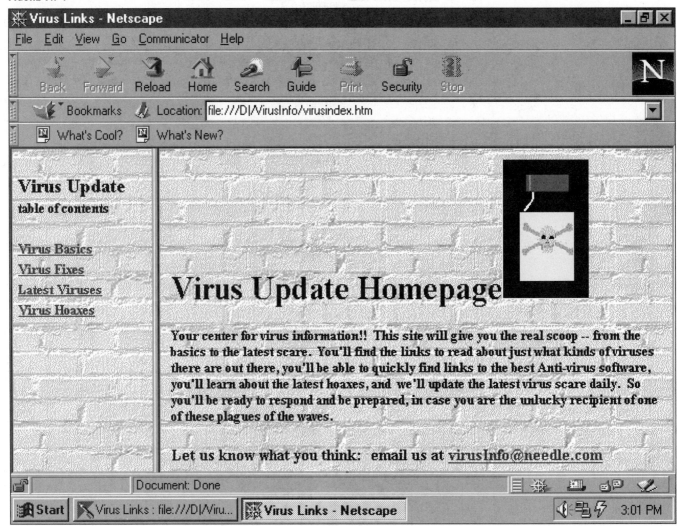

► ## Creating Web Sites Projects

Travel Web Site

In This Unit You Will:

 ► ## Create the Site Framework

 ► ## Insert an Image Map and Find Images

► ## Develop an Online Form

The international character of the World Wide Web makes it the perfect forum for sharing travel-related information. Users can visit commercial travel sites to book airline flights, reserve hotel accommodations, and rent cars. In addition, online travel guides such as those sponsored by Fodors and the Lonely Planet provide users with extensive tourism and travel-related information. You can contribute to the wealth of travel information already on the World Wide Web by creating an interactive travel site on a country or location that interests you. ►You have been asked by a friend who loves to travel in Japan to design a Web site that provides users with easy-to-find information about Japan and includes an online form for gathering their feedback. You will set up a framed site that includes an image map with active links to information about five major cities in Japan. In addition, you will create a form that users can complete to send their comments and questions.

PROJECT 1

OVERVIEW

Japan Travel Site

Your goal is to create a visually exciting travel site about Japan that users will want to visit to obtain travel-related information, share their own travel experiences, and request additional information. Ultimately, this site will provide links to information on five major cities in Japan: Tokyo, Sapporo, Kyoto, Osaka, and Kobe. Initially, it will contain a framed home page, an image map, and active links to information about the city of Kyoto. Three projects are required to complete the Web site:

Project 1

Creating the Site Framework

In Project 1, you will create the framework for the Web site. The site contains seven pages and a table of contents. You will create each of the seven pages in the site as illustrated in the storyboard in Figure O1-1; however, you will include content on only four pages: the home page (main.htm), the Table of Contents page (toc.htm), the page that provides travel information about Kyoto (kyoto.htm), and the page that includes an online form (form.htm). In addition, you will create the index.html page that contains the HTML codes for the frames. Links to the remaining pages will appear in the table of contents, but the linked pages will not contain information—as yet. Web site designers often develop the framework for a Web site, launch the site on the World Wide Web, and then make additions to the site over time. Figure O1-2 displays the completed index page with the table of contents displayed in a horizontal frame at the bottom of the screen.

Project 2

Inserting an Image Map and Developing the Kyoto Page

An image or interactive map contains "hot spots." When a user clicks a hot spot, the page relating to the link appears. In the image map illustrated in Figure O1-2, users can click on each of the five cities to go to the related page. Once you have inserted the image map of Japan, you will search the World Wide Web to find a variety of images to enhance the Kyoto page.

Project 3

Developing an Online Form

In Project 3, you will create an online feedback form that users can fill in with information about their own travel experiences or to obtain further information about travelling to Japan.

FIGURE 01-1: Web site storyboard

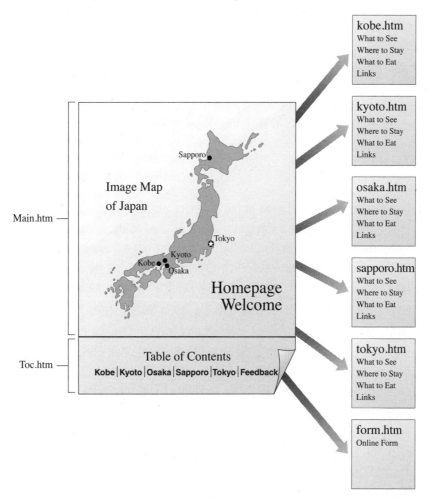

FIGURE 01-2: Home page for the Japan travel site

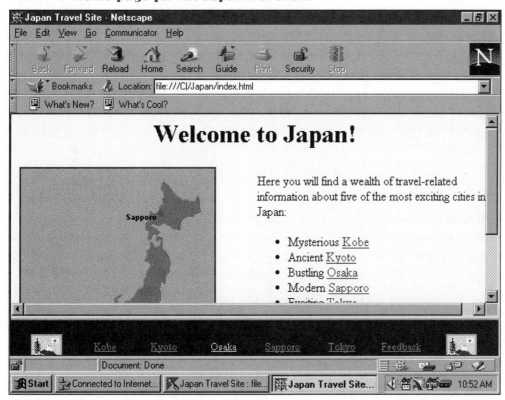

CREATING THE SITE FRAMEWORK

Three activities are required to create the framework for the Japan travel Web site: **Set Up the Site**, **Create the Remaining Pages**, and **Create the Frames**.

activity:

Set Up the Site

To set up the Japan travel site, you need to create a folder to store all the files for the site, obtain image files from the Creating Web Sites Illustrated Projects Student Online Companion, choose the background and font colors that you want to appear on every page in the site, then create the home page (main.htm), and the Kobe page (kobe.htm).

steps:

1. Create a folder called **Japan** in the directory where you store the files for this book, connect to the Internet, start **Netscape Navigator**, click in the **Location text box** on the Navigator toolbar, type **www.course.com**, press **[Enter]**, scroll down the page that appears, click the **Jump list arrow**, click **Student Online Companions**, click <u>Creating Web Sites Illustrated Projects</u>, right click the file **japan.htm** under Unit E, click **Save Link As**, display the **Japan folder**, then click **Save**

2. Save the following files for Unit E to the Japan folder: **japan.gif** and **scene.jpg**

   Next, you will open Netscape Composer and select the background and font colors.

3. Click the **Composer button** 🖉 on the Components bar, click **Format** on the menu bar, click **Page Colors and Properties**, click the **Colors and Background tab**, click the **Color Schemes list arrow**, click **Black on Lt. Yellow** as shown in Figure P1-1, then click **OK**

   Next, you will enter a heading for the page, and then save it as main.htm.

4. Press **[Ctrl][E]** to turn on centering, type **Welcome to Japan!**, enhance it with the **Heading 1 style**, click the **Save button** 💾 on the Composition toolbar, type **main**, click **Save**, enter **The Japan Travel Site** as the page title, then click **OK**

   Next, you will adapt the page and save it as kobe.htm.

5. Select the word **Japan**, type **Kobe**, click **File** on the menu bar, click **Save As**, type **kobe**, then click **Save**

   To save time, you will set up the Kobe page with the headings and targets that you want to appear on each page in the Web site that describes a city (e.g., Kyoto, Tokyo, etc.), so that you can use the Kobe page to create the remaining pages. You will first create a table below the heading that contains the links to four headings that you will designate as targets.

6. Press **[Enter]** after the heading **Welcome to Kobe!**, click the **Table button** 🖽 on the Composition toolbar, press **[Tab]**, type **4** for the number of columns, click **OK**, complete the table as shown in Figure P1-2, then enter the four headings from **What to See** to **Links** and format them as shown in Figure P1-2

7. Click to the left of **What to See** in the list of headings, click the **Target button** 🎯 on the Composition toolbar, type **see**, click **OK**, then create the following targets from the remaining headings:

Heading	Target Name
Where to Stay	stay
What to Eat	eat
Links	links

8. Select the text **What to See** in the table, click the **Link button** 🔗 on the Composition toolbar, click **see** in the Select a name list, click **OK**, then create the required links to the **stay**, **eat**, and **links** targets

   The Kobe page appears, as shown in Figure P1-3.

9. Click 💾 on the Composition toolbar

   Next, you will go on to use the kobe.htm file to create the pages for each of the remaining four cities and then to create the table of contents page and the Form page.

Hint

If the Page Title dialog box does not appear, click Format, click Page Colors and Properties, click the General tab, enter the title of the page, then click OK.

FIGURE P1-1: Colors and Backround tab

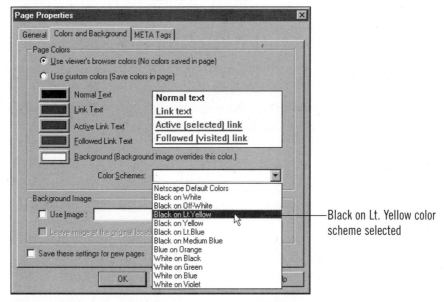

Black on Lt. Yellow color scheme selected

FIGURE P1-2: Table and text for the Kobe page

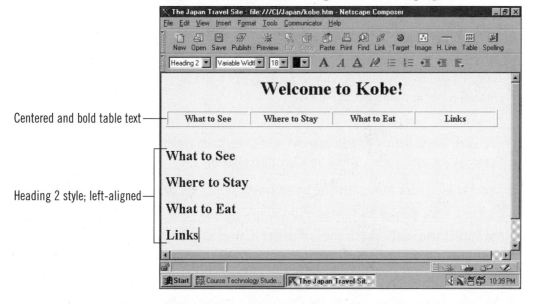

Centered and bold table text

Heading 2 style; left-aligned

FIGURE P1-3: Completed Kobe page

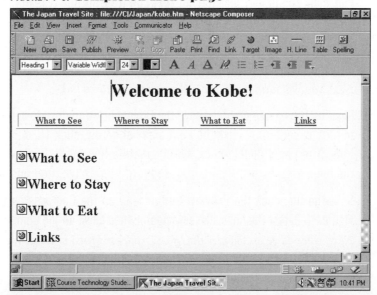

PROJECT 1

CREATING THE SITE FRAMEWORK

activity:

Create the Remaining Pages

In the previous activity, you set up the Kobe page with the text and links that you want to appear on the pages that will display information about Kyoto, Osaka, Sapporo, and Tokyo. Now you need to save the Kobe page under the name of each of the remaining cities, create the feedback form page, and then create the Table of Contents page.

steps:

1. Select the word **Kobe**, type **Kyoto**, save the file as **kyoto.htm**, select the word **Kyoto**, type **Osaka**, save the file as **osaka.htm**, then make the required replacements and save the next two pages as follows:

Text	Filename
Welcome to **Sapporo**	Save as **sapporo.htm**
Welcome to **Tokyo**	Save as **tokyo.htm**

   The Tokyo page appears, as shown in Figure P1-4. You have created the framework for the first six pages in the Japan travel site. Next, you will create the page that will contain the online form you will create in Project 3.

2. Open the file **main.htm**, select the text **Welcome to Japan!**, type **Share Your Travel Tips**, press **[Enter]**, type **or Ask Questions**, apply the **Heading 1** style, then save the file as **form.htm**

   Next, you will create a table of contents for the Japan travel site. The table of contents will appear in a separate frame at the bottom of the screen.

3. Click the **New button** on the Composition toolbar, click **Blank Page**, click **Format** on the menu bar, click **Page Colors and Properties**, click the **Colors and Background tab**, click the **Color Schemes list arrow**, click **White on Blue**, then click **OK**

4. Save the file as **toc.htm**, enter **The Japan Travel Site** as the page title, then click **OK**

5. Click the **Table button** on the Composition toolbar, enter **8** for the number of columns, click the **Border line width check box** to deselect it, then click **OK**

   Next, you will insert a stylized picture of Japan in column 1. This image will be designated as a link to the main page.

6. Click the **Image button** on the Composition toolbar, in the Image location area click **Choose File**, click **scene.jpg**, click the **Alt. Text/Low Res. button**, type **Home**, click **OK**, click the **Link tab**, click **Choose File**, click **main.htm**, click **Open**, then click **OK**

7. As shown in Figure P1-5, reduce the size of the image, enter the text for each cell in the table, then copy the image and paste it into the eighth cell in the table

   Next, you will format the text and create the required links.

8. Position the mouse pointer above the table, click and drag to select the entire table, press **[Ctrl][E]** to turn on centering, click the **Font Size list arrow**, click **10**, double-click **Kobe**, create a link to the **kobe.htm** page, double-click **Kyoto**, create a link to the **kyoto.htm** page, then create the links to the remaining pages: **osaka.htm**, **sapporo.htm**, **tokyo.htm**, and **form.htm**

9. Save the file, click the **Preview button** on the Composition toolbar, compare your screen with Figure P1-6, test the links, close Navigator, then close all the Composer pages except the toc.htm page

   Next, you will go on to enter the HTML codes required to create frames for the Table of Contents page.

FIGURE P1-4: Tokyo page

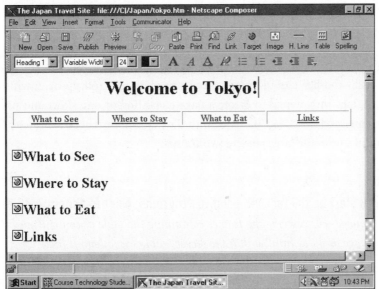

FIGURE P1-5: Completed table

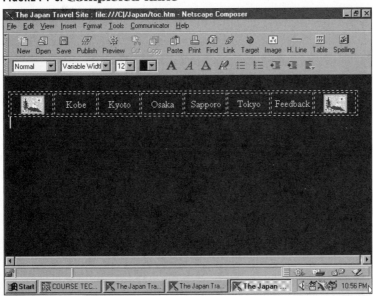

FIGURE P1-6: Table of Contents page in Navigator

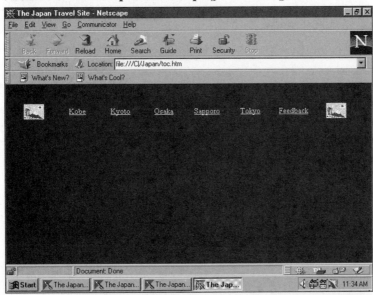

activity:

Create the Frames

You want the table of contents visible at all times so that users can either return to the main page or go "visit" another city in Japan without needing to scroll up or down the page. You will first enter HTML tags in Notepad to create a page consisting of one short and one tall horizontal frame, and then enter an HTML tag in the toc.htm file that will instruct the browser to display whatever page the user links to in the larger of the two frames.

steps:

1. Click **Start** on the taskbar, point to **Programs**, point to **Accessories**, then click **Notepad**

This page will describe the frames containing the table of contents and the main pages. You will save the page as index.html so that the server will know to load it first.

2. Click File on the menu bar, click **Save**, open the **Japan folder**, type **index.html**, then click **Save**

Next, you will enter the HTML tags to set up the index.html page with frames.

Hint

Remember to press [Tab] to indent the code where indicated.

3. Maximize the screen, then enter the HTML tags exactly as shown in Figure P1-7

4. Verify that you have typed the text correctly

5. Click **File**, click **Save**, click the **Close button**, then display **Netscape Composer**

Next, you will display the framed site.

Hint

If the links are cut off in the bottom frame, display the toc.htm file and reduce the size of the images.

6. Click the **Open button** 🔲 on the Composition toolbar, click **index.html**, click **Open**, then click the **Preview button** 🔲

The framed site appears, as shown in Figure P1-8. Next, you will enter an HTML tag in the toc.htm file so that when users click a link in the Table of Contents frame, the linked page will open in the frame above.

7. Display the **toc.htm** page in Composer, click above the table, click **Insert** on the menu bar, click **HTML Tag**, type **<base target="main">**, click **Verify**, then click **OK**

A tag icon appears in the page. Next, you will test the new target.

8. Click **File**, click **Save**, close Notepad, display Composer, click 🔲, double-click **index.html**, click 🔲, then click **Sapporo**

The Sapporo page appears in the top frame, as shown in Figure P1-9.

9. Check each link in the table to verify that the frames and links work correctly, then close all the Navigator windows

Next, you will go on to Project 2 where you will add text to the main page and insert an image map, then develop the content for the Kyoto page.

FIGURE P1-7: **HTML tags entered in Notepad**

Press [Tab] to indent these lines —

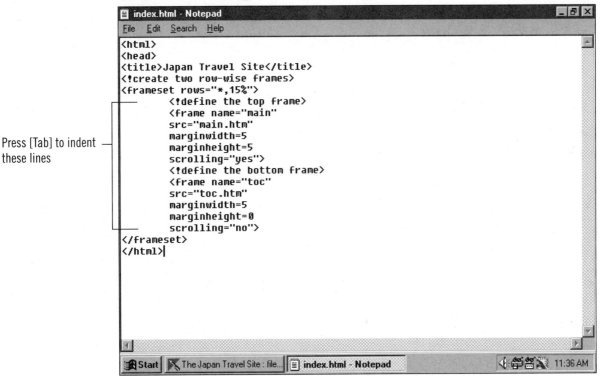

```
<html>
<head>
<title>Japan Travel Site</title>
<!create two row-wise frames>
<frameset rows="*,15%">
        <!define the top frame>
        <frame name="main"
        src="main.htm"
        marginwidth=5
        marginheight=5
        scrolling="yes">
        <!define the bottom frame>
        <frame name="toc"
        src="toc.htm"
        marginwidth=5
        marginheight=0
        scrolling="no">
</frameset>
</html>
```

FIGURE P1-8: **Framed site**

FIGURE P1-9: **Sapporo page displayed in Navigator**

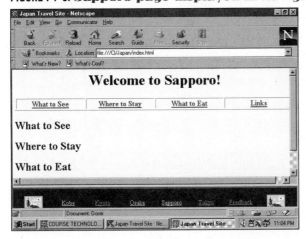

INSERTING AN IMAGE MAP AND DEVELOPING THE KYOTO PAGE

You have decided to provide visitors to your site with two ways to access information about each of the five cities. Visitors can click the links in the table of contents in the bottom frame or they can click the city on an interactive map of Japan. In this project you will Insert an Image Map, Develop Content for the Kyoto Page, and Find and Insert Images and Links.

activity:

Insert an Image Map

For this activity, an image map has already been developed. All you need to do is insert it in the main page and add alternate text.

steps:

1. Open the **main.htm** file, click after the heading, press **[Enter]**, click the **Table button** on the Composition toolbar, accept the default number of rows (1) and columns (2), click the **Border line width check box** to deselect it, then click **OK**

Next, you will open the japan.htm file that you saved from the Creating Web Sites Illustrated Projects Student Online Companion. This file contains the image map of Japan which you will copy into the Main page.

2. Open the **japan.htm** file, click **Edit** on the menu bar, click **Select All**, click the **Copy button** on the Formatting toolbar, display the **Main** page, then click the **Paste button**

The map of Japan appears in cell 1 of the table, as shown in Figure P2-1. Next, you will test the links from the map of Japan to the pages in the Japan travel site.

3. Click the **Preview button** on the Composition toolbar, click **Yes** to save the page, click the **red dot** next to **Sapporo**, click the **Back button** on the Navigator toolbar, click the **red dot** next to **Kobe**, click , test the links to **Osaka**, **Kyoto**, and **Tokyo**, then click **OK** to accept the error message indicating that the Tokyo page cannot be found

As you can see, the link to Tokyo does not work. You need to check the HTML tag for the Tokyo link to determine the problem.

4. Display the **main.htm page** in Composer, then point to the **third HTML tag** from the left to display the text, as shown in Figure P2-2

The HTML tag contains the map coordinates for Tokyo, the name of the file (toky.htm), and the name of the link (Tokyo). The name of the file is incorrect! You need to edit the HTML tag to change toky.htm to tokyo.htm.

5. Double-click the **third HTML tag** from the left, change **toky.htm** to **tokyo.htm**, then click **OK**

6. Save the file, click , test the link to the Tokyo page, then close Navigator

Next, you'll add alternate text to the map. This text will appear on browsers that do not display images and will also appear when a user of Netscape Communicator points the mouse at the map.

7. Display the **main.htm** page, right-click the **map**, click **Image Properties**, click **Alt. Text/Low Res.**, type **Image Map of Japan**, click **OK**, then click **OK**

Next, you will add text to the table in the main page.

8. Press **[Tab]** to move to the right column of the table, enter and format the text shown in Figure P2-3, then create links from each list item to the appropriate city page, and from the feedback form item to the form page

9. Save and close the **main.htm** file, display the **index.html** page, view it in Navigator, test the links you created, then close Navigator

Next, you will go on to develop the content for the Kyoto page.

FIGURE P2-1: Image map of Japan

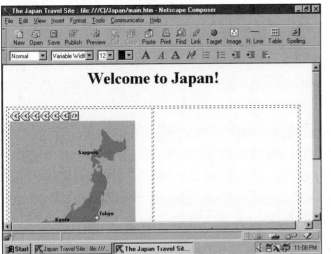

FIGURE P2-2: HTML tags in the Main page

FIGURE P2-3: Text for the Main page

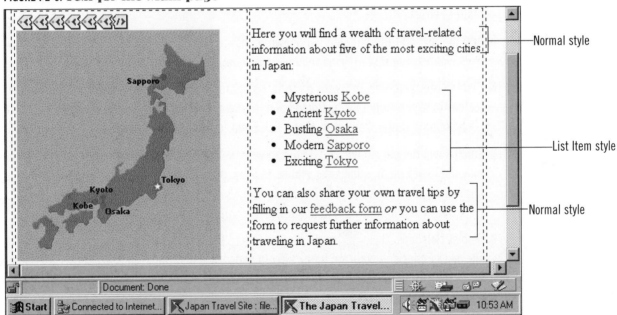

Here you will find a wealth of travel-related information about five of the most exciting cities in Japan: — Normal style

- Mysterious Kobe
- Ancient Kyoto
- Bustling Osaka
- Modern Sapporo
- Exciting Tokyo

— List Item style

You can also share your own travel tips by filling in our feedback form *or* you can use the form to request further information about traveling in Japan. — Normal style

Clues to Use

Creating an Image Map

To create an image map, you can use a shareware program such as LiveImage that you download from the World Wide Web. Check the Credits and Resources page in the Creating Web Sites Illustrated Projects Student Online Companion for a link to the LiveImage download site.

Web Sites

PROJECT 2

activity:

Develop Content for the Kyoto Page

To develop the content of the Kyoto page, you will search the World Wide Web for information about Kyoto, and then copy and paste selected text.

steps:

1. Open the file **kyoto.htm** in Composer, click the **Navigator button** on the Components bar, click **File** on the menu bar, click **Open Page**, type **city.net**, then press **[Enter]**
   In a few moments, the city.net site appears.

2. Click in the **Take me there text box**, type **Kyoto**, click the **Take me there button**, click <u>Kyoto</u>, <u>Japan</u>, click <u>Travel and Tourism</u> under Web Sites, then click <u>Kyoto-Convention City</u>
   The Kyoto-Convention City page looks like one you may want to use later in your development of the Kyoto site, so you decide to bookmark it before continuing your search for useful information.

3. Click the **Bookmarks button**, click **Add Bookmark**, scroll down the Kyoto-Convention City page, then click <u>Welcome to Kyoto</u>
   You can use some of the text on this page in the What to See section of your Kyoto page.

4. Select the text as shown in Figure P2-4, press **[Ctrl][C]**, display the **kyoto.htm** page in Composer, click after **What to See**, press **[Enter]**, press **[Ctrl][V]**, then correct any spacing, spelling, or grammatical errors

5. Add the text and the bulleted list shown in Figure P2-5
   Next, you need to find information about accommodations in Kyoto.

6. Display the **Welcome to Kyoto page** in Navigator, click the **Back button** on the Navigation toolbar to return to the Kyoto-Convention City page, click again to return to the city.net page, click <u>Lodging</u> under Web Sites, then click <u>Fodor's Hotel Index - Kyoto</u>

7. Scroll down the page, click **Hotel Fujita Kyoto**, select the text as shown in Figure P2-6, copy it, display the **Kyoto page**, click after **Where to Stay**, press **[Enter]**, paste the contents, then apply bold formatting to the text **Hotel Fujita Kyoto**
   Next, you will find information about where to eat in Kyoto.

Hint

Remember to press [Enter] after the What to Eat heading, to create a new paragraph for the restaurant information.

8. Display Netscape, click to display the Fodor's list of hotels, click again to display the city.net site, click <u>Fodor's Restaurant Index - Kyoto</u> under Food and Drink, click <u>Azekura</u>, copy the information about this restaurant, paste it below **What to Eat** on the Kyoto page, then enhance the text **Azekura** with bold formatting

9. Save the **kyoto.htm** file
   Next, go on to insert three images and then to create remote links to a variety of Kyoto travel sites.

FIGURE P2-4: Text selected on the Welcome to Kyoto page

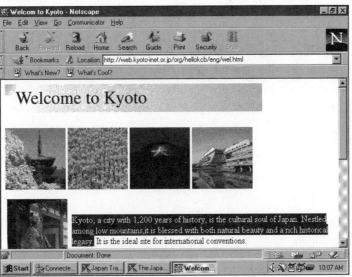

FIGURE P2-5: Text for the What to See page

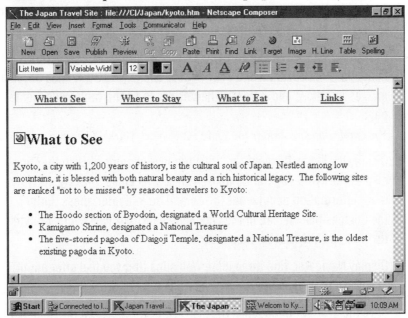

FIGURE P2-6: Hotel information selected

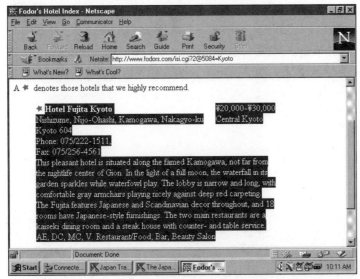

activity:

Find and Insert Images and Links

You will save three images from a Kyoto travel site on the World Wide Web, insert them in the Kyoto page, then develop links to a variety of Kyoto travel sites.

steps:

1. Display Navigator, click the **Bookmarks button** on the Location toolbar, click **Kyoto Convention Bureau Home Page**, scroll down the page, then click **Cultural Heritage**

Next, you will save a picture from the Cultural Heritage page, then insert it on the Kyoto page in Composer.

2. Right-click the first **picture** that appears, click **Save Image As** as shown in Figure P2-7, display the **Japan folder**, select the filename, type **kyoto1**, then click **Save**

3. Choose two more pictures from the Cultural Heritage page or from other pages in the Kyoto-Convention City site and save them in the Japan folder as **kyoto2** and **kyoto3**

4. Display the **Kyoto** page in Composer, click below the What to See section, click the **Heading Style list arrow**, click **Normal**, then create a table consisting of three columns and 1 row

5. Click the first **cell** in the table, click the **Image button** 🖼️ on the Composition toolbar, under Image location click **Choose File**, double-click **kyoto1.gif**, click **OK**, insert your **kyoto2** and **kyoto3** images in cells 2 and 3, resize the images to fit the table cells, center each image, then save the page

Your table appears similar to Figure P2-8. Next, you will complete the Links section of the Kyoto page.

6. Display the **Kyoto-Convention City page** in Navigator, click in the **Location text box**, press **[Ctrl][C]**, display the **Kyoto page** in Composer, click after **Links**, press **[Enter]**, type **Follow these links to find more information about what to see and do in Kyoto:**, press **[Enter]**, click the **Link button** 🔗 on the Composition toolbar, in the Link Source text box type **Kyoto-Convention City**, click in the **Link to text box**, press **[Ctrl][V]**, then click **OK**

7. Display Navigator, find three more Web sites that you feel offer an interesting range of information about Kyoto, then create the required links in the Kyoto page

8. Save the **kyoto.htm file**, click the **Preview button** 🔍 on the Composition toolbar, test your remote links, then close Navigator

The bottom section of the Kyoto page will appear similar to Figure P2-9. Next, go on to Project 3, where you will create a form that visitors to the Japan travel site can fill in to share their own travel experiences or to request additional information.

FIGURE P2-7: Saving an image in Navigator

FIGURE P2-8: Table with images inserted

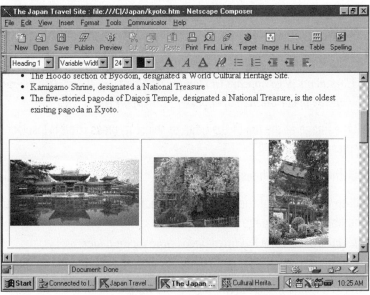

FIGURE P2-9: Bottom section of the Kyoto page

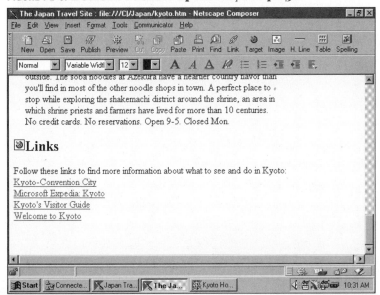

 PROJECT 3

DEVELOPING AN ONLINE FORM

You want to provide visitors to the Japan travel site with the opportunity to share their own travel experiences or to request additional information. On the form page, you will create a form for users to fill in. You can use several methods to create an online form. You can insert the appropriate HTML tags, you can create an online form in a program such as Microsoft Word 97, or you can borrow and then adapt a form from an existing page on the World Wide Web. This last method is the easiest and fastest, provided you can find a form that appears similar to the form you wish to include on your Web site. In Project 3, you will Borrow and Adapt a Form and then Modify the HTML Tags.

activity:

Borrow and Adapt a Form

You will first display the feedback page on one of the Kyoto travel sites and then save the page as a file in Composer. Then you will delete the elements on the page that you don't want to include on your page and copy the remaining text and HTML tags to the form.htm file.

steps:

Hint

If you are not able to display the city.net page for Kyoto, type "www.city.net" in the Location text box, press [Enter], type "Kyoto" in the Take me there! text box, click the Take me there! button, click Travel and Tourism under Web Sites, then click Welcome to Kyoto.

1. Display Navigator, click the **Back button** on the Navigation toolbar until the city.net page for Kyoto appears, click <u>Travel and Tourism</u> under Web Sites, then click <u>Welcome to Kyoto</u>
A Kyoto travel page sponsored by Stanford University appears.

2. Scroll to the bottom of the page, then click <u>**Comments**</u>, as shown in Figure 3-1

3. When the Comments page appears, click **File** on the menu bar, then click **Edit Page**
The Comments page appears in Composer. Next, you will delete the sections of the form that you do not want to appear on the Form page in the Japan travel site.

4. Click the image at the top of the page to select it, press [**Delete**], select the text shown in Figure P3-2, then press [**Delete**]

5. Select the horizontal lines, text, and HTML tags shown in Figure P3-3, then press [**Delete**]

6. Scroll to the bottom of the page, then select and delete all the text and images from <u>**DISCLAIMER**</u> to the bottom of the page
Next, you will save the modified page in the Japan folder.

7. Click **File**, click **Save As**, open the **Japan folder**, type **feedback** as the filename, then click **Save**
Next, go on to modify the HTML tags so that the final form meets the requirements of the Japan travel site.

FIGURE P3-1: Welcome to Kyoto page in Navigator

FIGURE P3-2: Text selected

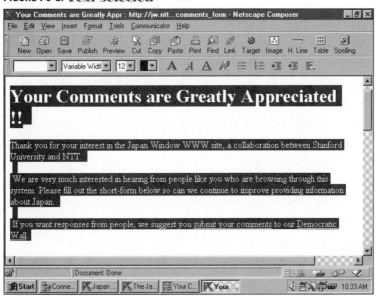

FIGURE P3-3: Text and HTML tags selected

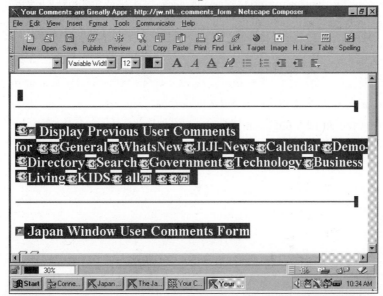

activity:

Modify the HTML Tags

The form that you borrowed contains some HTML tags that you do not need and some HTML tags that you need to modify. Your first step is to view the form in Navigator so you can see what changes you need to make.

steps:

1. Click the **Preview button** 🔳 on the Composition toolbar, then click the **list arrow** as shown in Figure P3-4

A list of options for the user to select appears. You have decided that you want only two options to appear: Personal Experience and Information. You therefore need to replace the existing options with these two options. You also need to add some text above the form to instruct the user and delete the options you do not require.

If the text appears in a long column, click after the word "Please," then press [Delete].

2. Click the **list arrow**, display the **Feedback page** in Composer, select the word **for**, and type **Please select Personal Experience if you want to share your own travel experiences in Kyoto or Information if you require further travel-related information about Kyoto**, then press **[Enter]**

3. Enhance the terms **Personal Experience** and **Information** with bold, double-click the word **General** and type **Personal Experience**, double-click **WhatsNew** and type **Information**, then select everything from the tag before **JIJI-News** to **KIDS**, as shown in Figure P3-5

4. Press **[Delete]**, save the file, click 🔳, then click the **list arrow** to view the two options

The form is developing nicely. Next, you will copy this form information to the form.htm file.

Make sure that you do not select the HTML tag following KIDS.

5. Display the **Feedback page** in Composer, click **Edit** on the menu bar, click **Select All**, press **[Ctrl][C]**, close the Feedback page, open the **form.htm** file in Composer, click after the word **Questions**, press **[Enter]**, then press **[Ctrl][V]**

Next, you'll add a Submit button at the bottom of the page that users will click to send the information in the form to the Internet Service Provider (ISP) that carries the Japan travel site.

6. Press **[Ctrl][End]** to move to the bottom of the page, press **[Enter]**, click **Insert** on the menu bar, click **HTML Tag**, type
<INPUT TYPE="button" VALUE="Submit"onClick="runSubmit(this.form, this)">, click **Verify**, then click **OK**

7. Click **Insert** on the menu bar, click **HTML Tag**, type **</INPUT>**, click **Verify**, then click **OK**

8. Save the file, display the **index.html** file, click 🔳, click **Feedback** in the Table of Contents frame, click the **list arrow**, compare your screen with Figure P3-6, scroll down the page, click the **Submit button**, then click **OK** to remove the error message

The Submit button does not send the form because the Japan travel site is not connected to an ISP. When you create a Web site that is carried by an ISP, you can request directions regarding the procedures required to activate the Submit button.

9. Check the various pages in the Japan travel site, close all the Navigator and Composer windows, then exit Netscape Communicator

FIGURE P3-4: Form with options displayed

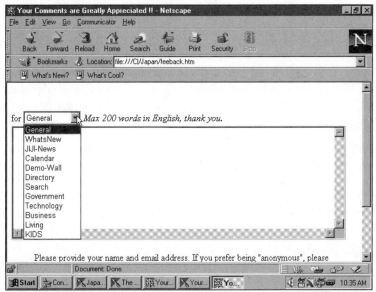

FIGURE P3-5: HTML tags selected

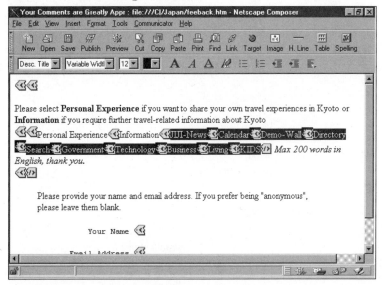

FIGURE P3-6: Completed form in Navigator

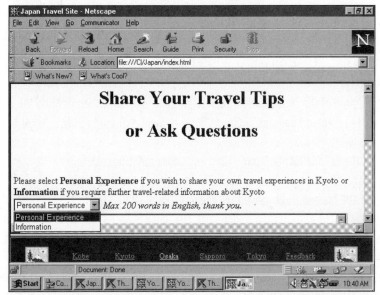

Independent Challenges

INDEPENDENT CHALLENGE 1

Create a travel-related Web site that provides information about a travel destination of your choice. The goal of the Web site is to provide users with information about an area of the world that you would either like to visit or that you are already familiar with. Your completed Web site should include at least five pages: a home page, a table of contents page, at least two pages describing specific locations in the travel destination you selected, and a page containing a feedback form. Follow the steps provided to organize your thoughts and create the Web site.

1. Select a travel destination that includes at least two locations. For example, you could create a travel site for Quebec and include a page describing Montreal and a page describing Quebec City, or you could create a travel site for Peru and include a page describing Lima and a page describing Machu Picchu. In the box below, write the name of your travel site and the two (or more) locations your site will cover:

Travel Site Destination:
Location 1:
Location 2:
Location 3 (optional):
Location 4: (optional):

2. Use the table below to organize your site.

Page Content	Filename
	main.htm

3. Use the table below to define the structure of two horizontal frames:

Top Frame	Bottom Frame
Name=	Name=
Width=	Width=
Height=	Height=
Contents (Source)=	Contents (Source)=
scrollable=	scrollable=

4. Create a folder for saving all the files associated with your travel Web site, then display Netscape Composer and create the background and color for the main page.
5. Save the main page under the name of the first location page (e.g., montreal.htm), then develop the structure of the location page. You should include links to targeted headings such as "What to See," "Where to Stay," "What to Eat," and "Links." Select different heading names, if you want.
6. Save the first location page as the second location page (and any subsequent pages).
7. Create the Table of Contents page, then create links to each of the pages in the Web site.
8. Create the HTML in Notepad for the framed page. Save this page as "index.html". (*Hint:* To reuse the HTML you created in this unit, open the index.html file you saved in the Japan folder, click File, click Save As, save the index.html file in the folder you created for your own travel site, then edit the HTML with your new variables.) For example, you might want to display the table of contents in the top frame and the main page in the bottom frame.
9. In Composer, insert an HTML tag in the table of contents page that targets the correct frame for display. (*Hint:* Remember to preview the site and check that all the links work properly.)

INDEPENDENT CHALLENGE 2

Now that you have created the framework for your travel site, you need to develop at least one of the location pages.

1. Search the Internet for a map of your destination, then save it and insert it in the main.htm file. (*Hint:* If you are able to download programs, you can create your own image map. Check the LiveImage link in the Credits and Resources page of the Creating Web Sites Illustrated Projects Online Companion.)
2. Develop appropriate text for the Main page. You want to welcome users to your site and inform them about the information they will find.
3. Search the Internet for information about your travel destination, then develop at least one of the location pages.
4. Include at least two pictures on each page you develop. Your goal is to create an attractive page that users will want to visit to find information about your travel destination.
5. Include a selection of links on each location page to other resources on the World Wide Web.
6. Preview all the pages in Navigator, and test all the remote links.

INDEPENDENT CHALLENGE 3

You need to borrow a form from a World Wide Web site and then adapt it for your Web site.

1. Check several of the travel sites related to your destination to find a site that includes an online form. Note that you can usually find an online form by clicking "feedback" or "comments" at the bottom of a travel site home page.
2. Display the form in Navigator. Click File on the menu, and then click Edit Page.
3. Delete all the HTML tags and text that you do not want.
4. Modify selected HTML tags until you are satisfied with the completed form. Frequently check the form in Navigator to monitor your progress.
5. Insert a Submit button at the bottom of the form page. The HTML tag required is:
   <INPUT TYPE="button" VALUE="Submit"onClick="unSubmit(this.form, this)">
6. Preview all the pages in your Web site in Navigator, make any adjustments required to the content or links, publish your site if possible, and then close Netscape Communicator. If you are not able to publish your site, print a copy of each page.

INDEPENDENT CHALLENGE 4

After a thrilling cruise to Alaska, you have decided to share your experiences with the world by creating a six-page Web site that includes a table of contents, an image map of Alaska, an online form, a description of Juneau—one of the cities you visited on your cruise—and two under-construction pages. Illustrated below is the outline for the Alaska Cruise site:

Page Content	Filename
Table of contents: illustrated in the top frame	toc.htm
Image map of Alaska Description of site	main.htm
Cruise ship description: under construction	ship.htm
Juneau description	juneau.htm
Ketchikan description: under construction	ketch.htm
Online form	form.htm

Follow the steps provided to complete the Web site for the Alaskan Cruise site.

1. Create a folder called "Alaska", display the Creating Web Sites Student Online Companion, then copy the files listed under Independent Challenge 4 for Unit E to the Alaska folder. The filenames are: alaska.gif, alaska.htm, comments.htm, heli.jpg, jackhammer.gif, mback.gif, tback.gif, and ship.gif.
2. Open a blank page in Composer, select the mback.gif image as the page background, select appropriate page colors, save the file as "main.htm", enter "Cruisin' Alaska" as the page title, enter "An Alaskan Cruise Vacation" as the heading, save the file again, then change the heading and save the file four more times as follows:

Heading	Filename
Luxury on the Sea	ship.htm
Wonderful Juneau	juneau.htm
Exciting Ketchikan	ketch.htm
Share Your Comments	form.htm

3. Create a new file called "toc.htm", select the tback.gif image as the background, then create a table with the links to the Main, Cruise Ship, Juneau, Ketchikan, and Comments pages.

4. Display Notepad, enter the HTML codes as shown below, then save the file as index.html.

```
<HTML>
<FRAMESET rows="15%,*">
<FRAME name="toc"
      src="toc.htm"
      marginwidth=5
      marginheight=5
      scrolling="no">
<FRAME name="main"
      src="main.htm"
      marginwidth=5
      marginheight=5
      scrolling="yes">
</FRAMESET>
</HTML>
```

5. Open the index.html page in Composer, click the Preview button to check the appearance of the site, open the toc.htm page in Composer, then add the HTML tag: <BASE TARGET="main">

6. Reload the index.html page in Navigator and check to ensure that the links from the Table of Contents frame work correctly.

7. Open the alaska.htm file, click Edit on the menu bar, click Select All, click the Copy button, open the file main.htm, create a table with two columns, click in column 1, click the Paste button, develop the Main page as shown in Figure IC-1 (make the ship picture a link to ship.htm), save the page, open the file index.html, then view it in Navigator.

FIGURE IC-1: Main and TOC pages viewed in Navigator

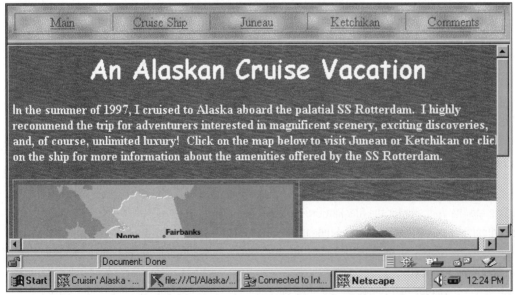

8. Insert the jackhammer.gif image and the text "Under Construction: Check Back Soon" in the ship.htm and ketch.htm files.

9. Open the juneau.htm file, then develop the Juneau page as shown in Figure IC-2. Note that you need to follow the directions in square brackets to find the required content.

FIGURE IC-2: Completed Juneau page

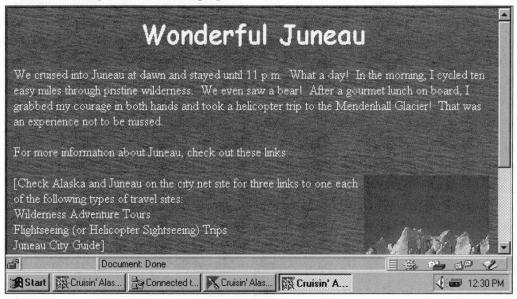

10. Open the comments.htm file, copy the contents of the page to the form.htm file, then modify the form so that, when viewed in Navigator, it appears as shown in Figure IC-3.

FIGURE IC-3: Completed form in Navigator

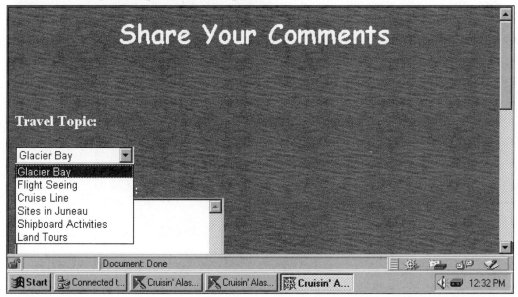

11. View the completed Alaska travel site in Navigator, print a copy of the Main, Juneau, and Form pages, then exit Netscape Communicator.

Visual Workshop

You need to adapt a form for Travel Tips, an online travel information site. Create a folder called "Workshop E", display the Creating Web Sites Illustrated Projects Student Online Companion, then save the following files listed under Visual Workshop for Unit E: form.htm and stars.gif. Open the file form.htm in Composer, add the background file (stars.gif), change the text colors, add "Travel Tips Feedback" as a Heading 1 title, then enter the options for the continents and travel categories as follows:

Continents: Africa, Europe, North America, Asia

Travel Categories: Accommodations, Tours, Sightseeing

Save the file, then view it in Navigator. The bottom section of the form should appear as shown in Figure VW-1.

FIGURE VW-1: Completed form in Navigator

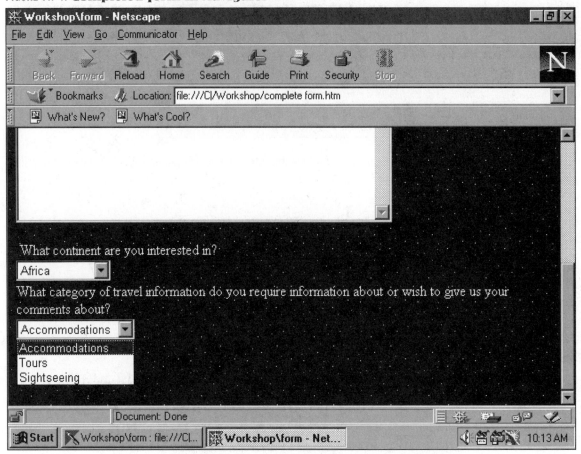

► ## Creating Web Sites
Projects

Online Business Web Site

In This Unit You Will:

 ► # Build Complex Tables

 ► # Create an Interactive Form with JavaScript

 ► # Add Special Effects with JavaScript

An online business Web site can generate income by selling services or products to customers far from its geographic location. It can also offer free products or services to attract potential customers to the site and keep them from surfing to competitive sites. Offering something for free is a highly effective advertising mechanism that enormously increases a company's visibility. ► In this unit, you will learn how to create a Web site that provides surfers with photographic images they can download free of charge and an easy way to order custom images for a fee. You will learn how to incorporate JavaScript into your site to enhance interactivity and add special effects.

PROJECT 1

World Photography

Brian Edmonds is a photojournalist who travels all over the world to capture his images. Brian has decided to display a selection of his photographs online for surfers to download free of charge. In addition, he wants to offer an image-finding service. Surfers who want an image of a specific locale or subject can complete Brian's online form and pay a small fee to receive an electronic copy of the image via e-mail. Figure O1-1 illustrates the storyboard for Brian Edmonds' World Photography Web site. The home page contains a picture of Brian along with images of photographs that represent five categories: animals, flowers, landmarks, landscapes, and people. Five linked pages display photographs in these categories, along with information about locations and subject matter. In addition, the home page links to a special request page that contains an interactive form for ordering photographs of images not available on the site. You will complete three projects to build Brian's World Photography Site.

Project 1

Building Complex Tables

In Project 1, you will create a complex table on the home page to contain a description of the site, a picture of Brian, images representing each of the subject categories, and text links to each category page and the request form. Figure O1-2 displays the completed home page for Brian's World Photography Site. You will then create each page in the site and develop the landscape category page.

Project 2

Creating an Interactive Form with JavaScript

In Project 2, you will copy a form that exists on the Web and modify it to fit the purposes of the World Photography Web site. You will then add JavaScript to the request form so that it includes interactive messages to the user.

Project 3

Adding Special Effects with JavaScript

In Project 3, you will use JavaScript to create a special visual effect on the home page. You will insert a banner that displays a constantly scrolling list of the image categories contained on Brian's Web site. The banner appears at the top of the page in Figure O1-2.

FIGURE 01-1: World Photography Web site storyboard

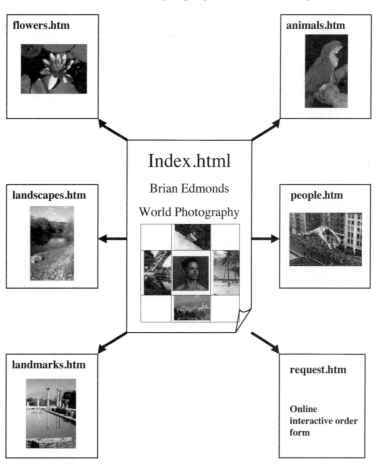

flowers.htm

animals.htm

landscapes.htm

Index.html

Brian Edmonds

World Photography

people.htm

landmarks.htm

request.htm

Online
interactive order
form

FIGURE 01-2: Homepage for the World Photography Web site

Banner

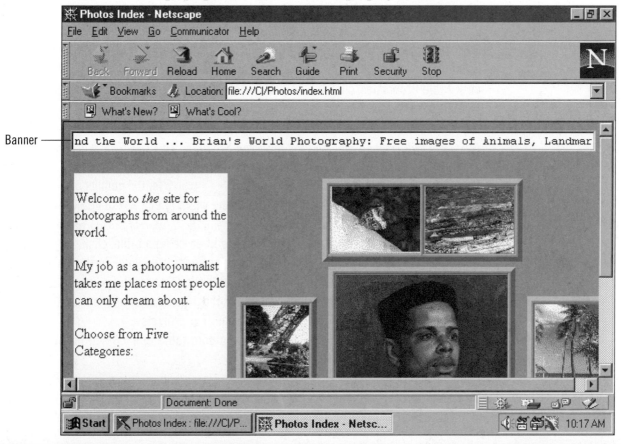

Four activities are required to build a complex table on the World Photography site home page and then set up the site: Create the Home Page, Complete the Table, Set Up the Category Pages, and Develop the Landscape Page.

activity:

Create the Home Page

Your first task is to create a folder for this Web site and then copy the files you will need from the Creating Web Sites Illustrated Projects Student Online Companion. Then you will set up the table that contains all the information and images you will display on the home page.

steps:

1. Create a new folder called **Photos**, connect to the Internet, start **Netscape Navigator**, press **[Ctrl][O]**, type **course.com**, click **Student Online Companions**, click the link for **Creating Web Sites Illustrated Projects Student Online Companion**, right-click the link for **brian.jpg** under Unit F, click **Save As Link**, then save it to the Photos folder

2. Save the following files to the Photos folder: **banner.htm**, **butter.jpg**, **eiffel.jpg**, **home.gif**, **lily.jpg**, **logs.jpg**, **maeght.jpg**, **paradise.jpg**, **redrock.jpg**, **sooke.jpg**, **sunset.jpg**, **superman.jpg**, **tropic.jpg**, and **village.jpg**, then disconnect from the Internet and close the Navigator window

3. Start **Netscape Composer**, click **Format** on the menu bar, click **Page Colors and Properties,** click the **General tab** if necessary, in the Title text box type **World Photography Site**, click the **Colors and Background tab**, click the **Color Schemes list arrow**, click **Black on Medium Blue**, click the **Normal Text color box**, click the **dark blue** in the sixth row, second column from the right, click the **Link Text color box**, click the **bright pink** in the fourth row, far right column, click the **Save these settings for new pages check box** to select it, then click **OK**

4. Click **File** on the menu bar, click **Save**, type **index.html**, then click **Save**

   Next, you will create a table consisting of two columns, then designate the size and color of the first column, which will contain text about the site.

5. Click the **Table button** 🔲 on the Composition toolbar, accept the default number of rows and columns, click the **Border line width check box** to deselect it, click **OK**, right-click the **first cell**, click **Table Properties**, click the **Cell tab** if necessary, click the **Cell width check box**, press **[Tab]**, type **30**, click the **Use Color color box** as shown in Figure P1-1, click the **light yellow** in the top row, fourth column, then click **OK**

   Next, you will create a table within the second column. This sub-table will consist of 3 rows and 3 columns and will contain further sub-tables that display images.

6. Press **[Tab]** to move to the second column, click 🔲, type **3** for the number of rows, press **[Tab]**, type **3** for the number of columns, click the **Border line width check box** to deselect it, then click **OK**

   Next, you will create a 2-column table within the middle column of the top row of the 3-column table.

7. Press **[Tab]** to move to the second column of the three-column table, click 🔲, accept the default number of rows and columns, click the **Center option button**, click in the **Border line width text box** to select it, delete the 1 and type **5**, compare your screen with Figure P1-2, then click **OK**

8. Click in the **bottom cell** of the middle column of the 3-column table, then create another **2-column table** that is **centered** and has a border line width of **5 pixels**

9. As shown in Figure P1-3, insert a **1-row**, **1-column table** in each cell in the middle row of the 3-column table

   Note the alignment directions in Figure P1-3. Next, you will go on to fill the complex table you have created with the required text and images for Brian's home page.

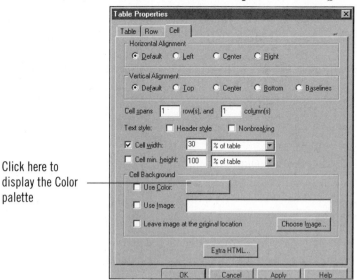

FIGURE P1-1: Table Properties dialog box

Click here to display the Color palette

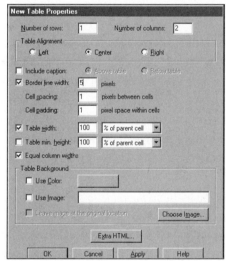

FIGURE P1-2: New Table Properties dialog box

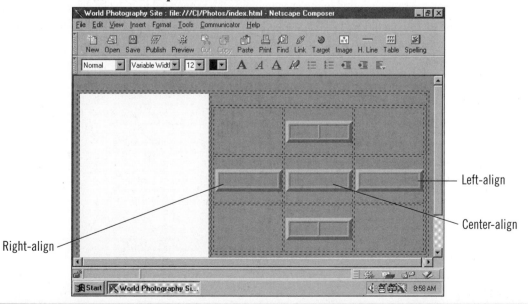

FIGURE P1-3: Completed tables

Right-align

Left-align

Center-align

activity:

Complete the Table

You need to insert information that introduces the site in the first column of the main table, and then insert images in all the sub-tables.

steps:

1. Click in the **first column** (the yellow column), then enter the text as shown in Figure P1-4

Next, you'll insert images into the tables.

2. Click in the **first cell** in the 2-column sub-table you inserted in the first row, middle column

3. Click the **Image button** 🖼 on the Composition toolbar, under Image Location click **Choose File**, open the **Photos folder**, double-click **butter.jpg**, then click **OK**

4. Press **[Tab]**, click 🔲, then insert the **logs.jpg** image

Compare your screen with Figure P1-5. Next, you will need to resize the two images.

5. Right-click the **butterfly image**, click **Image Properties**, double-click 142 in the **Height text box**, type **75**, click **OK**, right-click the **logs image**, click **Image Properties**, change the height to **75 pixels**, then click **OK**

6. Click the table inserted in the second row of the first column, insert the **eiffel.jpg** image, right-click the **image**, click **Image Properties**, in the Dimensions area change the width to **75 pixels**, click **OK**, click the **image**, click the **Alignment button** 📧 on the Composition toolbar, then click the **Right button** ▤

Next, you will reduce the width of the table so that the eiffel image completely fills it.

7. Right-click the **eiffel image**, click **Table Properties**, click the **Table tab** if necessary, double-click in the **Table width text box**, type **75**, click the **list arrow** next to **% of parent cell**, click **pixels**, then click **OK**

8. Click the **table** inserted in the second row of the second column, insert the **brian.jpg** image, right-click the **image**, click **Table Properties**, designate the table width at **200 pixels**, then click **OK**

9. As shown in Figure P1-6, insert and modify the remaining three images, then save the page

Next, you will go on to set up the remaining six pages in the Web site and create local links.

FIGURE P1-4: Text for column 1

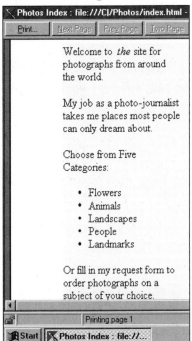

FIGURE P1-5: Images inserted in sub-table

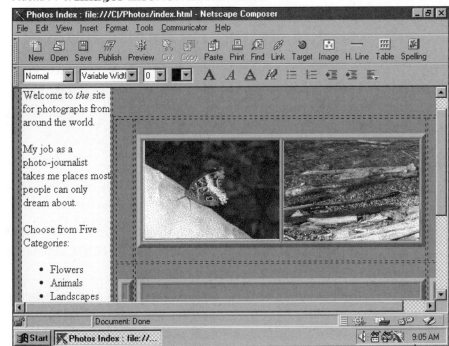

FIGURE P1-6: Sub-tables complete

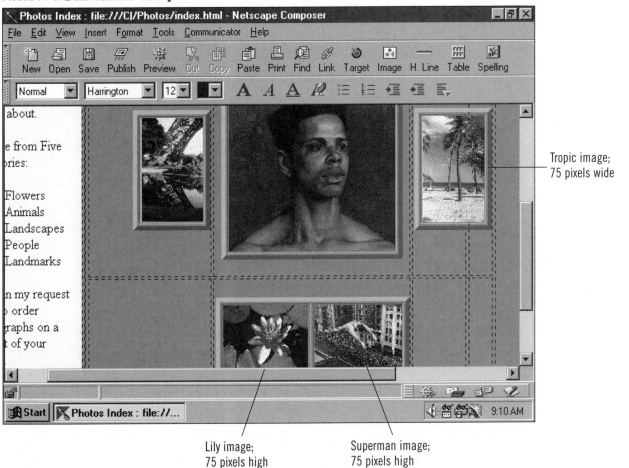

Tropic image;
75 pixels wide

Lily image;
75 pixels high

Superman image;
75 pixels high

activity:

Set Up the Category Pages

Your first task is to establish a framework for each of the five category pages in the Web site and then to save each page. You will then create local links from the home page and copy the links to the remaining pages in the Web site.

Hint

If the correct background color does not appear, display the Colors and Background dialog box, then select the Black on Medium Blue color scheme, dark blue for the normal text, and bright pink for the link text.

steps:

1. Click the **New button** on the Composition toolbar, click **Blank Page**, then create a table consisting of **1 row** and **2 columns** with no borders

2. Right-click **column 1**, click **Table Properties**, click the **Cell tab**, double-click in the **Width text box** and type **30%**, click the **Use Color color box**, click the **light yellow** in the first row, fourth column, then click **OK**

3. Press **[Tab]** to move to column 2, type **Animals**, select it, click the **Paragraph Style list arrow** on the Formatting toolbar, click **Heading 1**, press **[Ctrl][E]** to center the text, deselect the text, press **[Enter]**, create a table consisting of **3 rows** and **2 columns**, with a border line width of **5 pixels**, then click **OK**

4. Save the file as **animals.htm**, then enter **Brian's World Photography** in the Page Title dialog box
   Your screen appears as shown in Figure P1-7.

5. Select the word **Animals**, type **Flowers**, save the page as **flowers.htm**, then make the required changes and save three more pages as follows:

Heading	Filename
Landmarks	landmarks.htm
Landscapes	landscapes.htm
People	people.htm

6. Click , click **Blank Page**, save the page as **request.htm**, then enter **Request Page** in the Page Title dialog box
   You will complete the Request page in Project 2. Next, you will need to create local links from the home page to the six other pages in the Web site and then copy the links to the location pages.

7. Display the home page (**index.html**), double-click the text **Flowers** in column 1, click the **Link button** on the Composition toolbar, under Link to click **Choose File**, double-click **flowers.htm**, click **OK**, make links to the **animals.htm**, **landmarks.htm**, **landscapes.htm**, and **people.htm** files, then select the text **request form** and create a link to the **request.htm** file
   Next, you will copy the text and links from the main page to all the category pages.

8. Select the text as shown in Figure P1-8, click the **Copy button** on the Composition toolbar, open the **People page**, click in the **first column**, click the **Paste button**, click after the pasted text, then press **[Enter]** twice

9. Type **Home**, insert the **home.gif** image as shown in Figure P1-9, select the word **Home** and the image, click , create a link to the **index.html** file, right-click the **home image**, click **Image Properties**, under Space around images double-click in the **Solid Border text box** and type **0**, click **OK**, save the **people.htm** file, select all the text in column 1 and then copy and paste it into each of the remaining category pages: **animals.htm**, **flowers.htm**, **landmarks.htm**, and **landscapes.htm**, then save and close all the files except **landscapes.htm**
   Next, you will go on to develop the content for the Landscapes page.

FIGURE P1-7: **Animals page complete**

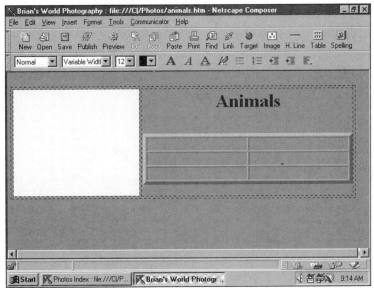

FIGURE P1-8: **Text selected**

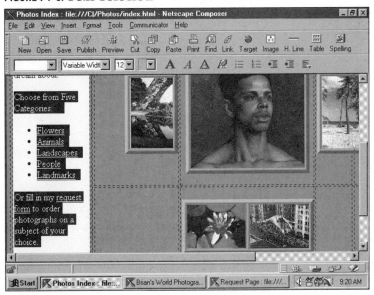

FIGURE P1-9: **Home text and image inserted**

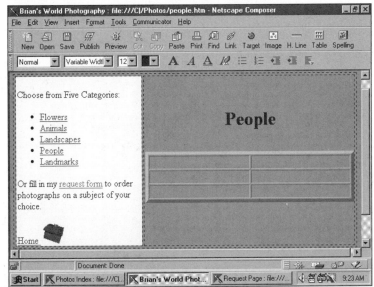

BUILDING COMPLEX TABLES

activity:

Develop the Landscapes Page

You will develop only the Landscapes page on Brian's World Photography Web site. However, once you have completed the Landscapes page, you may want to develop one or two of the other pages by inserting images of your own.

steps:

1. With the Landscapes page open on your screen, click in the **first cell** of the two-column table

2. Click the **Image button** 🖻 on the Composition toolbar, under Image Location click **Choose File**, double-click **sooke.jpg**, then click **OK**

3. Press [**Enter**]

4. Create a table consisting of **4 rows** and **2 columns** with no borders, click the **Use Color color box**, click the **light yellow** in the first row, fourth column, then click **OK**

5. Right-click the **first cell** in the main table, click **Table Properties**, click the **Cell tab**, set the cell width at **40%** of the table width, then click **OK**

6. Complete the table as shown in Figure P1-10

7. Insert the remaining images and create the required tables as shown in Figure P1-11
Remember to set the width of cell 1 in each table at 40%.

8. Right-click the **first column** in the main table (the table containing the links), click **Table Properties**, click the **Cell tab**, in the Vertical alignment area click the **Top option button**, then click **OK**

8. Save the file, preview it in Navigator, then close Navigator and close the landscapes.htm file
The Landscapes page appears similar to the one in Figure P1-12. Next you will go on to Project 2, where you will use JavaScript to develop an interactive form on the Request page.

Hint

You cannot copy and paste a table; therefore, you need to create each table separately.

FIGURE P1-10: Sooke information complete

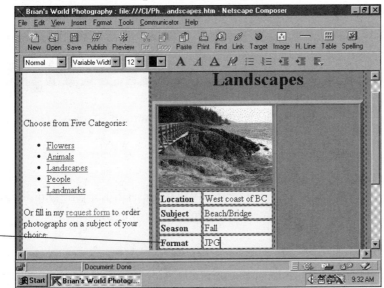

Format these — headings in bold

FIGURE P1-11: Images and tables complete

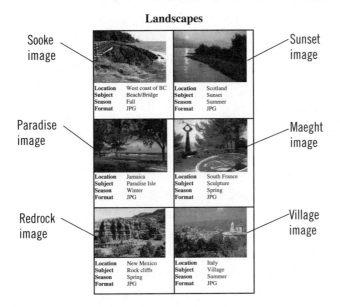

Sooke image

Sunset image

Paradise image

Maeght image

Redrock image

Village image

FIGURE P1-12: Landscapes page viewed in Navigator

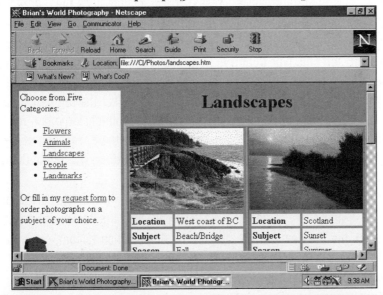

Web Sites

Creating an Interactive Form with JavaScript

In this project, you will: **Set Up the User Data, Set Up the Photo and Payment Data,** and **Add JavaScript.**

activity:

Set Up the User Data

Rather than type the HTML tags from scratch, you will use an automotive ordering form that contains some of the elements you want and customize it for your needs.

steps:

Hint

If you cannot locate the automotive page, open the Student Online Companion, then click Car Form under Unit F.

Hint

If your screen displays the message "The selection includes a table cell boundary. Deleting and copying are not allowed" appears, reselect the text without the paragraph marks.

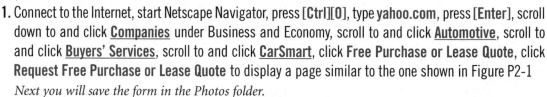

1. Connect to the Internet, start Netscape Navigator, press **[Ctrl][O]**, type **yahoo.com**, press **[Enter]**, scroll down to and click <u>Companies</u> under Business and Economy, scroll to and click <u>Automotive</u>, scroll to and click <u>Buyers' Services</u>, scroll to and click <u>CarSmart</u>, click **Free Purchase or Lease Quote**, click **Request Free Purchase or Lease Quote** to display a page similar to the one shown in Figure P2-1

   Next you will save the form in the Photos folder.

2. Click **File** on the menu bar, click **Edit Page**, press **[Ctrl][A]** to select the entire page, press **[Ctrl][C]**, open the file **request.htm**, press **[Ctrl][V]**, save the file, then disconnect from the Internet

3. Select the **image** at the top of the screen, press **[Delete]**, select the text (**Note: All fields are required**), then press **[Delete]**

   Next, you will modify the user information.

4. In the first cell of the left column of the table, select the word **Salutation** and type **E-mail Address**, select all the tags in the top cell of the right column, press **[Delete]**, scroll down to almost the bottom of the table, select the tag next to E-mail Address, press **[Ctrl][C]**, scroll back up to the top of the table, click in the cell next to E-mail Address, press **[Ctrl][V]**, select the tag you just pasted, click the **Paragraph style list arrow** on the Formatting toolbar, then click **Formatted**

   Next you will change the size of the EMAIL tag, so that the input box is smaller.

5. Double-click the **EMAIL tag**, select the text **42** after SIZE=, type **32**, select the text **42** after MAXLENGTH =, type **32**, click **OK**, then point to the tag and read the contents, as shown in Figure P2-2

6. Scroll to and click after the word **State**, type **/Province**, select all of the tags (for the 50 states) in the right cell, then press **[Delete]**, click the **tag** in the cell next to City to select it, press **[Ctrl][C]**, click in the cell next to State/Province, press **[Ctrl][V]**, double-click the **tag**, replace the word **CITY** with **STATE/PROV**, click **OK**, right-click **State/Province**, click **Insert**, then click **Row**

   You will add the alignment for the new row, type the label and modify a copied tag.

7. Click in the **empty left cell**, type **Country:**, right-click the text you just typed, click **Table Properties**, click the **Cell tab** if necessary, under Horizontal Alignment click the **Right option button**, under Vertical Alignment click the **Top option button**, click **OK**, select the tag next to City, press **[Ctrl][C]** click in the cell to the right of **Country**, press **[Ctrl][V]**, double-click the **tag**, replace the word **CITY** with **COUNTRY**, click **OK**, select the tag if necessary, click the **Paragraph style list arrow** on the Formatting toolbar, click **Formatted**, then click the **Save button** on the Composition toolbar

   Next you will delete some unnecessary rows.

8. Right-click **Daytime Phone Number**, point to **Delete**, click **Row**, then delete the rows containing **Evening Phone Number**, **E-mail Address**, and **How did you hear about the CarSmart Service?** in the same way

9. Click, click the **Preview button** on the Composition toolbar, compare your screen with Figure P2-3, then close Navigator

   Next, you will go on to modify the page so that users can order a photo.

FIGURE P2-1: CarSmart AutoFinder

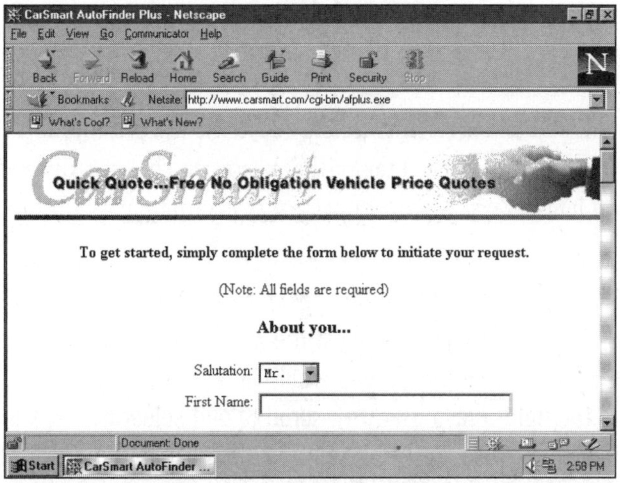

FIGURE P2-2: EMAIL tag modified

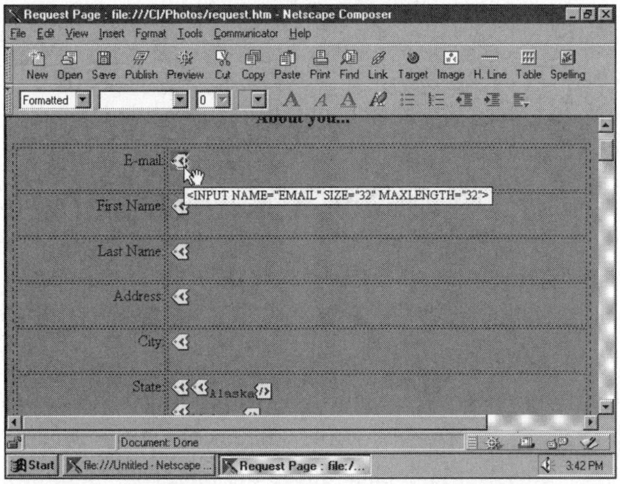

FIGURE P2-3: Preview of user information

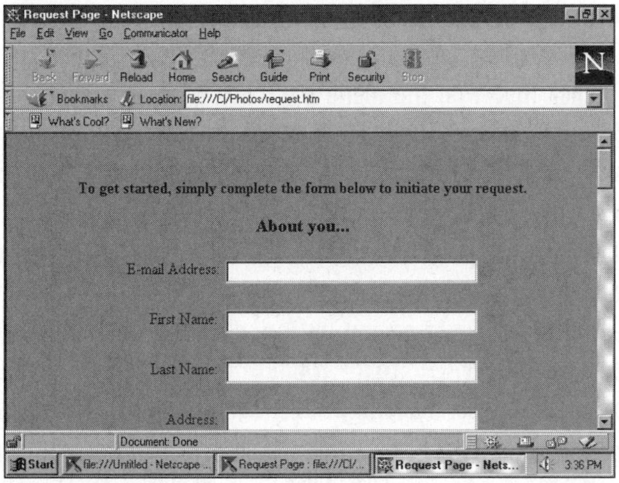

Clues to Use

Publishing Your Form

To publish your form on a server, you insert the name of the program or script after "ACTION" in the form tag. The ACTION is often a CGI (Common Gateway Interface) script, which is a custom program specific to the server platform. In this case, you won't modify the tag unless you know the specific action for your server.

activity:

Set Up the Photo and Payment Data

First, you will add text areas for users to describe the photograph they want and then you will modify the option values of a select tag so that users can choose from a wide variety of file formats. Finally, you will add labels, tags, and an image for collecting payment information.

steps:

1. Display the **request.htm** file in Composer, select the word **vehicle** in the sentence "About the vehicle you want...", type **photograph**, select the word **year** in the left cell of the first row of the second table, type **Describe the photograph you would like. Please be as specific as possible.**, select the **tags** in the cell to the right, press **[Delete]**, scroll to and select the **tags** in the cell to the right of "Additional Information:...", press **[Ctrl][C]**, scroll to and click in the right cell of the top row of the table, press **[Ctrl][V]**, double-click the first tag you inserted (the **TEXTAREA NAME tag**), select the text **MOREINFO**, type **PHOTO** as shown in Figure P2-4, then click **OK**

   Next, you will modify the select tags so users can request specific file formats.

2. Select the text **Vehicle Manufacturer**, type **File Format**, select the text **Acura**, type **JPEG**, select the text **Alfa Romeo**, type **GIF**, then continue to substitute the select list with file formats as shown in Figure P2-5

3. Delete the remaining text and its option tags (from **Eagle** to **Volvo**), but be sure to leave the final select tag as shown in Figure P2-5, click the **Preview button** [icon] on the Composition toolbar, click **Yes**, scroll to the File Format list, click the **select arrows**, notice that the size of the box increases to handle the longest file format name, Hewlett-Packard Graphics Language (.hgl), then close the Navigator window

   Next, you will delete unnecessary rows and add payment information.

4. Right-click the word **Model**, point to **Delete**, click **Row**, delete the rest of the rows in the table (through **Lease or Purchase?**) in the same way, click in front of the text **Payment Information (if purchasing)**, press **[Enter]**, click above the line, type **Each photo is only $10 in any file format you request!**, select the text, then click the **Italic button** [A] on the Formatting toolbar

5. Select the text **Payment Information (if purchasing)**, type **Credit Card Information**, select the text **Method of Payment**, type **Cardholder Name**, select the text and tags in the right cell, press **[Delete]**, click **Insert** on the menu bar, click **HTML tag**, type **<INPUT TYPE="text" NAME="Card Holder Name" SIZE=31 >**, click **OK**, select the text **Down Payment Amount**, type **Mastercard, VISA or Discovery #:**, delete the cell contents of the right cell, click in the right cell, click **Insert**, click **HTML tag**, type **<INPUT TYPE="text" NAME="CARDNUMBER" SIZE=31 >**, then click **OK**

6. Right-click the **cell**, point to **Insert**, click **Row**, click in the left cell, type **Expiration Date:**, right-click **Expiration Date**, click **Table Properties**, click the **Cell tab** if necessary, under Horizontal Alignment click the **Right option button**, click **OK**, click in the right cell, click **Insert**, click **HTML tag**, type **<INPUT TYPE="text" NAME="EXP" SIZE=11>**, click **OK**, select the text **Trade-in Information**, then type **...or fill in this form, print it, and mail with a check to:**

7. Select the text **Year:**, type **Brian Edmonds**, select the text **Make:**, type **25 Place du Trocadero**, continue to type the text as shown in Figure 2-6, right-click in any right cell, point to **Delete**, then click **Column**

8. Click just in front of the pair of tags below the table, click **Insert**, click **New Line Break**, double-click the **INPUT TYPE tag**, select the text **Continue..**, type **SUBMIT**, click **OK**, select the first link, type **Return to home page**, create a link for this text to the **index.html** file, then delete the remaining links at the bottom of the page

9. Click [icon], click **Yes** to save the changes, check the link to the home page, return to the Request page, compare your screen with Figure P2-6, then close the Navigator window

   Next, you will go on to add JavaScript for interactivity.

FIGURE P2-4: HTML Tag dialog box

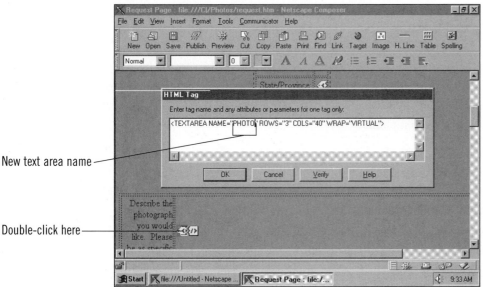

New text area name

Double-click here

FIGURE P2-5: File format select option values

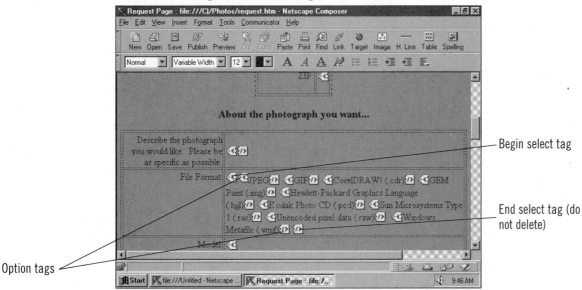

Begin select tag

End select tag (do not delete)

Option tags

FIGURE P2-6: Payment information with Submit button

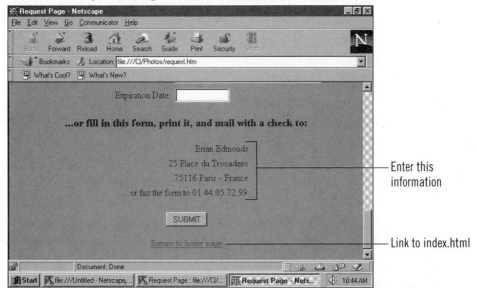

Enter this information

Link to index.html

CREATING AN INTERACTIVE FORM WITH JAVASCRIPT

activity:

Add JavaScript

Helpful tips, suggestions, and alerts can appear as users fill in forms by inserting JavaScript. For example, if a user moves to a field for a home phone number, an alert message could appear that reminds users that they can leave this field blank for security purposes. First, you will add JavaScript that greets the user by first name.

steps:

Hint

To establish the external editor, click Edit, click Preferences, then click Choose next to HTML Source to identify the editor of your choice. You can use Notepad or another editor, such as WordPad.

Hint

You can use the Edit HTML Source commands to edit code, or you can start Notepad and then open the file. Either method works.

1. Display the **request.htm** page in Composer, click **Edit** on the menu bar, click **HTML Source**, maximize the screen, click after **</TITLE>**, press **[Enter]**, then type the script as shown in Figure P2-7, pressing **[Tab]** to indent the lines

2. Scroll down to the line that begins **<FORM ACTION**, click in front of the word **ACTION**, type **NAME="Form"**, press **[Spacebar]**, scroll to the line beginning **<PRE><INPUT NAME="FIRST-NAME"**, click after **MAXLENGTH="32"**, press **[Spacebar]**, type **onBlur="hello()"**, compare your screen with Figure P2-8, click **File** on the menu bar, click **Save**, click the **Close button**, then click **Yes** to reload the page

3. Click the **Preview button** on the Composition toolbar, click in the box next to **First Name**, type **Muriel**, press **[Tab]**, read the message, click **OK**, then close Navigator

   *Next, you will add a JavaScript alert message. First, you will create a function called **warning**.*

4. Click **Edit**, click **HTML Source**, maximize the screen, scroll down to and click after **Each photo is only $10 in any file format you request!</I></H3></CENTER>**, press **[Enter]**, then type the following:
   <SCRIPT> //Custom function called warning to show message.
   function warning() {
   var msg= "Warning - This is not a secure site. If you"
   msg+= "are uncomfortable sending credit card information"
   msg+= "over the Internet, please feel free to use the"
   msg+= "postal system."
   alert(msg)
   }
   </SCRIPT>

   Next you will add the event handler, onBlur, that will initiate the warning.

5. Scroll down to and click after the line **<TD><INPUT TYPE="text" NAME="Card Holder Name" SIZE=31** of the **INPUT TYPE** for the cardholder's name, press **[Spacebar]**, type **onBlur="warning()"**, click **File**, click **Save**, click **Text Document** close Notepad, click **Yes**, click , click **Yes**, scroll to the credit card information, type **Muriel Marks** in the cell to the right of Cardholder Name:, press **[Tab]**, then view the message as shown in Figure P2-9

   You will edit the message to include spaces where appropriate.

6. Click **OK**, close Navigator, click **Edit**, click **HTML Source**, maximize the screen, scroll to the warning message you created just above the credit card information, click after the word **you**, press **[Spacebar]**, click after the word **information**, press **[Spacebar]**, click after the word **the**, press **[Spacebar]**, click **File**, click **Save**, click **Close**, click **Yes**, click , type **Muriel Marks** in the cell to the right of Cardholder Name:, press **[Tab]**, then view the message

Hint

Since this form isn't live on a server, you will see a message that Netscape is unable to locate the server.

7. Click **OK**, scroll to the top of the page, fill in the form with your personal information, then enter **A view of the cliffs and ocean at Etretat, France** for Photo 1, select the text **Unencoded pixel data (.raw)** for the file format, then enter your information for payment information

8. Click **Submit**, click the **Stop button** on the Navigator toolbar, then close the Navigator window

   Next, you will go on to Project 3 where you will add a scrolling banner to the top of Brian's home page.

FIGURE P2-7: JavaScript added to define hello function

Hello function defined ⎯

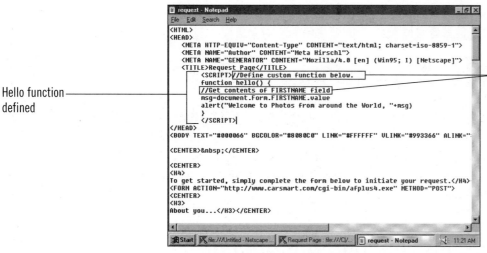

Comments (anything after //) explain the code, but are not interpreted by JavaScript

FIGURE P2-8: OnBlur action added

Form name defined ⎯

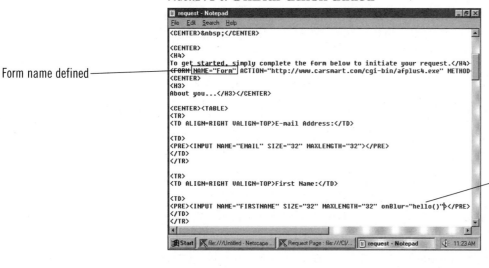

Hello function to start on Blur when cursor leaves the FIRSTNAME field

FIGURE P2-9: Alert message with missing spaces

Spaces missing ⎯

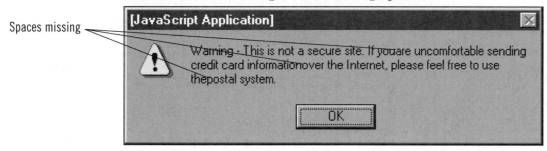

Clues to Use

Using Event Handlers

The tag for a text field on a form can contain event handlers that trigger JavaScript code in response to a user doing something to a field. For example, onBlur triggers JavaScript code when the cursor leaves the text box field while onFocus triggers JavaScript code when the cursor lands in the field.

Adding Special Effects with JavaScript

You can use JavaScript to add interesting special effects such as animations and sounds. In this project you will insert a banner at the top of Brian's World Photography Homepage. This banner will display continuously scrolling text to advertise Brian's site. To complete Project 3, you will: **Create and Enhance the Banner**. To create the banner, you will borrow the JavaScript from the banner.htm file you saved in Project 1.

activity:

Create and Enhance the Banner

steps:

1. Open the file **banner.htm** in Composer, click **Edit** on the menu bar, click **HTML Source**, maximize the screen, click **Edit**, click **Word Wrap**, then select all the text and codes from **<SCRIPT language="JavaScript">** to the code **</SCRIPT>** above the line **<BODY onLoad="ScrollBanner()">**, as shown in Figure P3-1

Next, you will copy the JavaScript you've selected to the index.html file so that you can then modify the JavaScript to display information about Brian's site.

2. Press **[Ctrl][C]**, minimize the Notepad window, then open the file **index.html**

3. Click **Edit**, click **HTML Source**, maximize the screen and turn on the **Word Wrap** feature, click after the **<HEAD>** tag, press **[Enter]**, then press **[Ctrl][V]**

4. Display the **banner.htm** file in Notepad, select the text and codes as shown in Figure P3-2, press **[Ctrl][C]**, display the Notepad screen for the index.html file, click after the line **<BODY TEXT="#000066" BGCOLOR="#8080C0" LINK="#FFFFFF" VLINK="#800080" ALINK="#FFFF00** (or similar codes), press **[Enter]**, then press **[Ctrl][V]**

5. Close the two Notepad windows (answering **Yes** to save the files), display the file **banner.htm** in Composer, click **Yes** to reload the file, close the **banner.htm** file, display the file **index.html** in Composer, click **Yes** to reload the file, then click the **Preview button** [icon] on the Composition toolbar

Next, you will further modify the index.html file so that you can add new text to the banner.

Hint

Make sure you don't delete the quotation mark (") following the three periods (...).

6. Close Navigator, display the **index.html** file in Composer, click **Edit**, click **HTML Source**, maximize the screen, turn on the Word Wrap feature, scroll down the page until you see **var msg1=" Brian's World Photography"**, click after the **y** in "Photography", type a **colon** (:), press **[Spacebar]**, then type **Free images of Animals, Landmarks, People, Flowers, and Landscapes from Around the World...**

7. Scroll down the page until you see the following lines:
**document.write('<form name="ScrollBanner"><input type="text" name="message" value="World Photography " size="75" pause()>
</form>');**

8. Change **World Photography** to **Brian Edmonds** so that the second line reads **value="Brian Edmonds " size="75" pause()>
</form>');**, close Notepad, click **Yes** to save the file, display the file **index.html**, click **Yes** to reload the page, then click [icon]

Your screen should appear similar to the one shown in Figure P3-3.

Hint

Delete the home image from the Landscapes page before you print the page.

9. Print a copy of the **home page**, the **Request page**, and the **Landscapes page** from Navigator, then close Navigator, then close Composer

FIGURE P3-1: Banner JavaScript selected

FIGURE P3-2: Banner position JavaScript selected

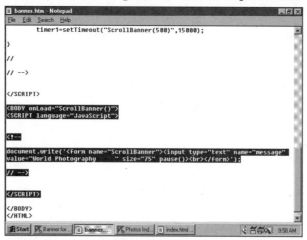

FIGURE P3-3: Completed home page in Navigator

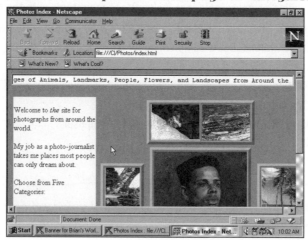

Clues to Use

JavaScript, HTML, and Java

You might be confused about the difference between JavaScript, HTML, and Java. JavaScript is a scripting language that is embedded in Netscape Navigator and Internet Explorer. JavaScript enables you to determine the way a page behaves, while HTML just determines how a page looks. Java is a complete stand-alone programming language, similar to C and C++, and requires third-party software such as a compiler to execute.

Independent Challenges

INDEPENDENT CHALLENGE 1

Create an online business Web site for a business of your choice. The site should display at least five images. You can use scanned images, if appropriate, or you can surf the World Wide Web and save images that match the requirements of your business site. For example, you could decide to create an online business site that sells books. You can find images of your favorite books by searching the World Wide Web for online bookstores and then copying images of the book covers.

1. Define your business in the box below:

Business Name	Products/Services

2. Use the table below to organize your site; make sure you include a form page:

Page Content	Filename
Home page	index.html

3. Create the home page (index.html) with a complex table that includes one main table with the table of contents in a full column at the side of the page or in a full row at the top of the page. Spend some time experimenting with inserting tables to display the images in an interesting and attractive manner. Use a complementary background and text color for the site and use it consistently across the site.
4. Create one of the pages using a selection of the images you have scanned or saved from World Wide Web sites. Create the links to the pages from the home page and then to the other pages.
5. Save the pages, preview them in Navigator, test each link, then return to Composer.

INDEPENDENT CHALLENGE 2

Create a form page with JavaScript for the online business site you created in Independent Challenge 1. The form will allow the user to e-mail questions and requests to you.

1. Connect to the Internet, and start a search engine such as Lycos, Yahoo, or AltaVista. Search for a form page in a business similar to yours by searching for the product and buy. For example, if your business sells bicycles, you would search on "Bicycles AND Buy". This will usually give you a list of sites that include a form for purchasing bikes. Alternatively, you could go through the categories in a service like Yahoo, and choose Companies and drill down to Buyers' Services. Once you find a form that contains most of the fields you want for your business, save it to the folder for your site.
2. Open the form, copy the entire page (press [Ctrl][A]), then paste it to the blank form page you created earlier. Modify the form in Composer to match your needs. Don't forget to change input type names if you copy and paste tags.
3. Insert JavaScript to give feedback to the user. You can use the script from Project 2 by modifying the text between the quotation

marks after alert. For example, the following script has been changed to add a message after a customer has entered the bicycle model number:

```
<SCRIPT>//Define custom function below.
      function verify() {
      //Get contents of bicycle model number
      msg = document.Form.MODELNO.value
      alert("The model you want is " +msg+". Is that correct?")
      }
</SCRIPT>
```

This function definition must appear before the head tag. Next add onBlur="verify()" to the input tag: Add NAME=Form to the form tag as you did in Project 2. You could also add the warning message if you accept credit card orders.

4. Test the script in Navigator. Then close Navigator and return to Composer. Add one more JavaScript interactive element to the form. You may want to alert customers to sending a credit card number over the Internet, or you may want to add a script that thanks customers for their business at the end of the form. Save the form.
5. Preview the form in Navigator, enter your own information to test the form, then print it, and close Navigator.

INDEPENDENT CHALLENGE 3

Add a banner to the home page you created in Independent Challenge 1.

1. Open the banner.htm file you saved in Project 3.
2. Display the HTML source, maximize the screen, and turn on the Word Wrap feature, copy the codes, then select all the text and codes from <SCRIPT language="JavaScript"> to </SCRIPT> above <BODY onLoad="ScrollBanner()">.
3. Press [Ctrl][C], minimize the Notepad window, then open your index.html file.
4. Click Edit on the menu bar, click HTML Source, maximize the screen and select Word Wrap, click after the <HEAD> tag, press [Enter], then press [Ctrl][V].
5. Display the Notepad window for the banner.htm file, then select the text and codes as shown in Figure IC-1:

FIGURE IC-1: Banner position JavaScript selected

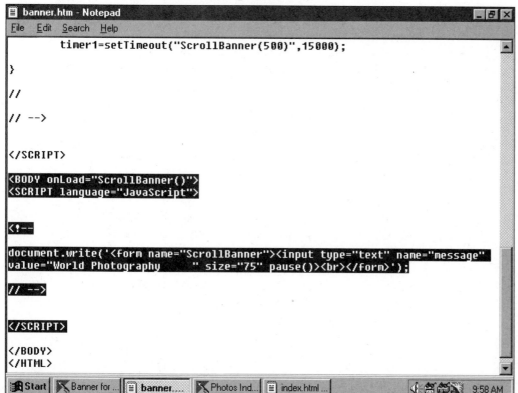

6. Press [Ctrl][C], display the Notepad window for the index.html file, click after the code for Body Text (begins "<BODY TEXT=" and includes the codes for the background and text colors you selected for the page), press [Enter], then press [Ctrl][V].

7. Close the two Notepad windows (answering Yes to save the files), display the file banner.htm in Composer, click Yes to reload the file, display the file index.html in Composer, click Yes to reload the file, then click the Preview button. The banner for Brian's World Photography site appears at the top of your screen. You need to change the text of the banner to match your online business.

8. Display the HTML source for the index.html file, scroll down the page until you see the text "var msg1=" Brian's World Photography"," then replace the text "Brian's World Photography" with the message you want to appear in the banner (for example, the name of your company).

9. Scroll down the page until you see the line that includes "value="World Photography"," then replace "World Photography" with the text you want to appear before the banner text (for example, the products or services your company sells); then save and close the Notepad file, reload the page, and preview your work.

10. Print a copy of the home page, the form page, and one or two of the other pages in your Web site, then close Navigator, close Composer, and exit Netscape Communicator.

INDEPENDENT CHALLENGE 4

To assist a friend who wants to sell her extensive collection of music CD's, cassettes, and vinyl recordings online, you will create a three-page Web site that includes a home page describing the various music categories, an online form, and a page that displays the recordings available in one of the categories you have selected (for example, Rare Jazz, Classic Rock, Underground Bands, etc.).

1. Create a folder called "Music," then create the file index.html so the page appears similar to Figure IC-2. You decide which background and text colors to select.

FIGURE IC-2: Sample home page for Arlene's Online Music Store

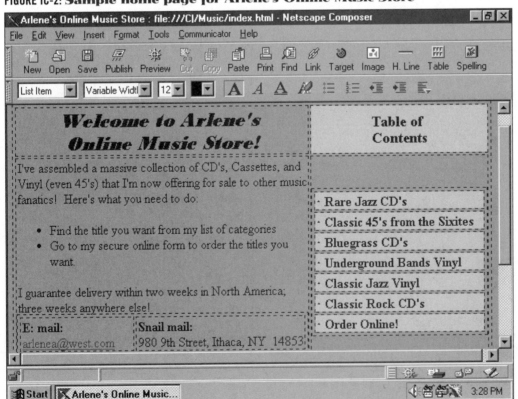

2. Create the Request page and link it to the home page.

3. Create a page for a category of your choice (e.g., Rare Jazz, Classic 45's, Bluegrass, etc.). Figure IC-3 provides you with a framework for the page. You need to list at least ten recordings on the page. If you want, expand the table to include images of the album/CD covers that you have downloaded from other music sites on the World Wide Web.

FIGURE IC-3: Sample category page for Arlene's Online Music Store

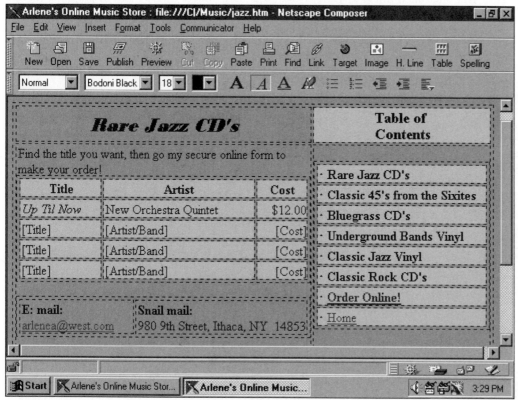

4. Open the Request page, then create an online form similar to the form you created in Project 2. Note that you can copy the codes from the form into the Request page, then make the required changes to the codes so that the finished form allows users to order a specific recording in a category of their choice. You decide how much you want to charge for each recording.

5. Add JavaScript to the form to make it interactive. For example, you can add an alert message that asks users if they have selected the correct recording category.

6. Test the form, then print the Request page.

7. Open the banner.htm file you created in Project 3, and copy the required codes to your home page. Modify the JavaScript so that the following message appears: "Arlene's Online Music Store...Order Hard-to-Find Titles at Great Prices . . ."

8. Modify the value= script to replace "World Photography" with "Arlene's Online Music Store."

9. Print a copy of the home page and the category page you developed, then close Composer, close Navigator, then exit Netscape Communicator.

Visual Workshop

The World Wide Web is chock-full of free images that you can use to create dynamic and attractive Web sites. If you download a number of images, you can sometimes forget which filename belongs to which image. To help you manage a selection of image files, you will create a Web site called Image Organizer that organizes images by type and displays the images in a table. Using Figure VW-1 as your guide, create the Web site in a folder called "Images." Download the background images for this Web site listed under Visual Workshop in Unit F in the Student Online Companion.

FIGURE VW-1: Background page of Image Organizer in Composer

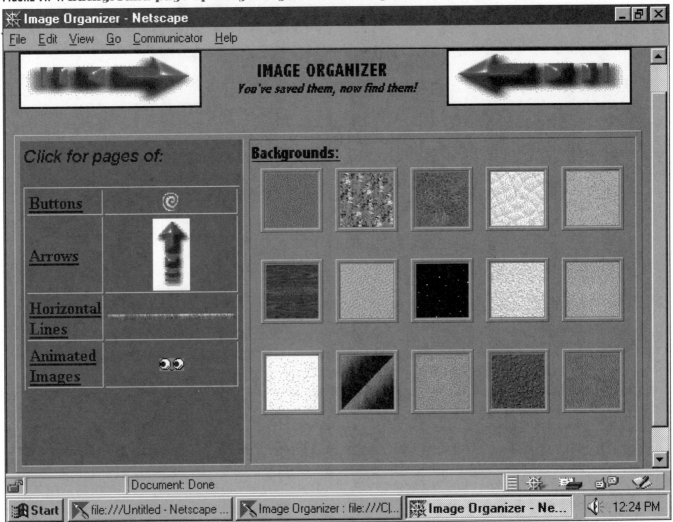

Index

►A

alert messages, JavaScript, *WS F-16-17*

alignment
  of images, *WS D-4, WS F-6*
  of tables, *WS F-4*
  of text, *WS A-10-11*

AltaVista, *WS A-16*

alternate images, *WS B-16-17*

Alternate Images Properties dialog
  box, *WS B-16-17*

alternate text
  for image maps, *WS E-10*
  for images, *WS B-16-17*

animated images
  effects of, *WS C-12*
  inserting, *WS B-8-9, WS C-14-15*
  JavaScript techniques, *WS F-18*

►B

backgrounds
  adding, *WS A-10*
  color, *WS E-4, WS F-8*
  custom, *WS A-11*
  in tables, *WS F-10-11*

banners, JavaScript for, *WS F-18-19*

"Best of the Web" sites, *WS C-19*

bitmap files, editing in Paint,
  WS B-14-15

blank pages, opening, *WS A-8*

Blinking option, *WS C-10*

bold text, *WS A-6*

bookmarks, *WS A-16*

border lines, for tables, *WS F-4*

browsers
  not supporting frames, *WS D-2*
  older, accommodating, *WS B-16*

bulleted lists, *WS A-4-5, WS A-6-7*
  indentation of, *WS D-6*

Bullet List button, *WS A-4, WS A-6,
  WS A-16*

bullets, removing, *WS A-16*

►C

cells
  color backgrounds in, *WS F-10-11*
  inserting images in, *WS E-14-15*
  width of, *WS F-4*

center alignment, for text, *WS A-10-11*

Character Properties dialog box,
  WS A-8, WS A-9
  Link tab, *WS C-12-13*

Check Spelling dialog box, *WS C-8*

classification names, adding,
WS C-18-19

clip art, *See also* images
inserting, WS A-14-15

color
backgrounds, WS E-4, WS F-8
of links, WS A-8, WS A-10-11,
WS C-6, WS F-4
table backgrounds, WS F-10-11
of text, WS A-10-11, WS C-6,
WS F-4

Colors and Backgrounds tab,
WS E-4-5

Comments page, creating form for,
WS E-16-19

community Web sites, WS C-1-19
adding targets, WS C-12-13
animated images in, WS C-12,
WS C-14-15
classification names for, WS C-18-19
framework for, WS C-6-7
home page content, WS C-8-9
local link page content, WS C-10-11
meta-information for, WS C-16-17
planning, WS C-2-3
reviewing similar sites, WS C-4-5
value of, WS C-1

Composer, starting, WS A-4-5

content
for community Web sites,
WS C-8-9, WS C-10-11
developing, WS C-8-11, WS E-12-13
for information Web sites,
WS D-6-7, WS D-14-15
for personal Web sites, WS A-2
for small business Web sites,
WS B-6-7
for travel Web sites, WS E-12-13

contents, tables of. *See* table of contents (TOC) page

copying text, into Composer, WS A-6

counters, inserting, WS B-18-19

credit cards, JavaScript alert message
for, WS F-16-17

custom backgrounds, WS A-11

► **D**

Decrease Indent button, WS D-6

deleting
links, WS B-18
styles, WS C-10

description, adding to meta-
information, WS C-16-17

design, consistency of, WS B-2

downloading, images, WS B-4-5,
WS E-14-15

► **E**

Edit HTML Source command,
WS F-16

editor, external, selecting, WS F-16

e-mail links, WS C-8
creating, WS A-18-19

event handlers, JavaScript, WS F-17

Excite, WS A-16

external editor, selecting, WS F-16

► **F**

Font Color list arrow, WS A-10

forms
adding text areas to, WS F-14-15
borrowing and adapting,
WS E-16-19
creating, WS E-16-17

creating option values for,
  WS F-14-15
input tags, *WS F-14-15*
JavaScript, interactive, *WS F-12-17*
for online business sites, *WS E-2*
publishing, *WS F-13*
viewing, *WS E-18-19*
frames
  alternatives for browsers not sup-
    porting, *WS D-2, WS D-16-19*
  creating, *WS E-8-9*
  defining size of, *WS D-9*
  HTML code for, *WS D-8-9*
  previewing, *WS E-8-9*
  targeting, *WS D-10-11*
  testing, *WS D-10*
  uses of, *WS D-6*
  using, *WS D-2*
  viewing, *WS D-8*
  viewing no frames pages in
    Composer, *WS D-18-19*
frameset tags, *WS D-9*
  value lists, *WS D-9*

►G

.GIF files, *WS A-14, See also* images
  animated, *WS B-8-9*
graphics. *See* images
greetings, by name, *WS F-16-17*

►H

Heading styles, *WS C-8, WS D-4*
  applying, *WS A-4, WS A-6,*
    WS B-10-11
hello function, JavaScript, *WS F-16-17*
hits, recording with counters,
  WS B-18-19

home page, for personal Web sites,
  WS A-4-5
Horizontal Line Properties dialog box,
  WS A-12-13
horizontal lines, *WS A-12-13*
  custom, *WS B-8-9*
  removing, *WS A-12*
hot spots, in image maps, *WS E-2*
HTML code
  adding comments to, *WS D-8*
  for browsers not supporting frames,
    WS D-16-19
  for counters, *WS B-18-19*
  editing, *WS F-16*
  for frames, *WS D-8-9*
  frameset tags, *WS D-9*
  JavaScript and Java vs., *WS F-19*
  modifying tags, *WS E-18-19*
  tag pairs, *WS D-8*
  tags for forms, *WS E-16-19,*
    WS F-14-15
  tags for frames, *WS E-8-9*
  target tags, *WS D-10-11*
  viewing source, *WS C-18-19*
.HTML extension, *WS A-4*
HTML Tag dialog box
  for counters, *WS B-18-19*
  for forms, *WS F-14-15*
  for targets, *WS D-10-11*

►I

image maps
  alternative text for, *WS E-10*
  creating, *WS E-11*
  defined, *WS E-2*
  inserting, *WS E-10-11*
Image Properties dialog box,
  WS B-4-5, WS F-6

images
  adding text to, *WS B-14-15*
  alignment of, *WS D-4, WS F-6*
  alternate (low resolution),
    WS B-16-17
  alternate text for, *WS B-16-17*
  animated, *WS B-8-9, WS C-12,
    WS C-14-15*
  for backgrounds, *WS A-10-11*
  bitmap files, *WS B-14-15*
  clip art, *WS A-14-15*
  custom horizontal lines, *WS B-8-9*
  downloading (saving), *WS B-4-5,
    WS E-14-15*
  file formats, *WS A-14*
  GIFs, *WS A-14, WS B-8-9*
  inserting, *WS A-14-15, WS B-4-5,
    WS B-12*
  inserting in tables, *WS E-14-15,
    WS F-6-7*
  JPG, *WS A-14*
  as links, *WS B-12-13*
  modifying in Paint, *WS B-14-15*
  properties, *WS A-14*
  sizing, *WS A-14, WS B-14*
  sources of, *WS E-5*
  wrapping text around, *WS A-14-15*
indentation, *WS D-6*
Index page
  creating, for small business Web site,
    WS B-4-5
  developing, for small business Web
    site, *WS B-8-9*
information Web sites, *WS D-1-19*
  finding and adding remote links,
    WS D-12-15
  HTML code for frames, *WS D-8-9*
  HTML for non-frame pages,
    WS D-16-19
  planning, *WS D-2-3*
  setting up, *WS D-4-5*
  table of contents page, *WS D-6-7,
    WS D-14-15*
  targeting frames, *WS D-10-11*
  value of, *WS D-1*
input tags, for forms, *WS F-14-15*
interactive forms, with JavaScript,
  WS F-2
interactive maps. *See* image maps
Internet service providers (ISPs)
  counters, *WS B-18*
  defined, *WS A-18*
  selecting, *WS A-19*
italic text, *WS A-6*

►J

Java, *WS F-19*
JavaScript
  creating interactive forms with,
    WS F-12-17
  defined, *WS F-19*
  event handlers, *WS F-17*
  for greeting users by name,
    WS F-16-17
  for interactive forms, *WS F-2*
  scrolling text banners, *WS F-18-19*
  for special effects, *WS F-2,
    WS F-18-19*
.JPG files, *WS A-14*

►K

keywords
  adding to meta-information,
    WS C-16-17
  multiple, *WS C-17*

►L

lines
  custom, *WS B-8-9*
  horizontal, *WS A-12-13*
Link button, *WS A-8, WS A-16*
links
  color of, *WS A-8, WS A-10-11,
    WS C-6, WS F-4*
  developing, *WS E-14-15*
  e-mail, *WS A-18-19, WS C-8*
  finding and inserting, *WS D-12-15*
  images as, *WS B-12-13*
  local, *WS A-8-9*
  remote, *WS A-8, WS A-16-17,
    WS D-12-15*
  removing, *WS B-18*
  targeted, *WS C-12-13*
lists, bulleted, *WS A-4-5, WS A-6-7*
LiveImage, *WS E-11*
local links
  creating, *WS A-8-9*
  defined, *WS A-8*
Location text box, *WS A-6*
low resolution images, as alternate
  images, *WS B-16-17*

►M

mailto: links, *WS A-18-19, WS C-8*
memory requirements, open windows
  and, *WS A-12*
meta-information
  adding description and keywords,
    WS C-16-17
  defined, *WS C-2*
  spelling in, *WS C-16*
Microsoft Word, copying text into
  Composer from, *WS A-6*

►N

names, greeting users by, *WS F-16-17*
Navigator button, *WS A-19*
Navigator windows, closing, *WS A-12*
New button, *WS A-8*
New Table Properties dialog box,
  WS D-17, WS F-5
non-frame pages, creating, *WS D-16-19*
Notepad, *WS C-4*
  creating HTML code for frames in,
    WS D-8-9, WS E-8-9
  creating HTML code for no frames
    in, *WS D-16-17*
  editing HTML in, *WS F-16*

►O

OnBlur function, JavaScript,
  WS F-16-17
online business Web sites, *WS F-1-19*
  category pages, *WS F-8-9*

creating tables, *WS F-4-7*
developing pages for, *WS F-10-11*
home page, *WS F-4-5*
JavaScript interactive forms,
    WS F-12-17
JavaScript special effects,
    WS F-18-19
planning, *WS F-2-3*
value of, *WS F-1*
option values, in forms, *WS F-14-15*

►P

Page Colors and Properties, Colors
    and Backgrounds tab, *WS E-4-5*
Page Properties dialog box
    background and text colors,
        WS A-10-11
    classification names, *WS C-18-19*
    home page description, *WS C-16-17*
    keywords, *WS C-16-17*
    page title, *WS C-6*
Page Source, viewing source code,
    WS C-18-19
Page Title dialog box, *WS A-4,
    WS A-5, WS B-4-5*
Paint, modifying images in, *WS B-14-15*
paragraphs
    creating, *WS E-12*
    heading style, *WS A-4, WS A-6,
        WS B-10-11, WS C-8, WS D-4*
Paragraph Style list arrow, *WS C-8,
    WS D-4*
personal Web sites, *WS A-1-19*
    background for, *WS A-10-11*
    developing content for, *WS A-2*
    e-mail links, *WS A-18-19*
    home page, *WS A-4-5*
    horizontal lines, *WS A-12-13*

images, *WS A-14-15*
local links, *WS A-8-9*
overview, *WS A-2-3*
publishing, *WS A-18-19*
remote links, *WS A-16-17*
resume page, *WS A-6-7*
skills and interest page, *WS A-8-9*
text colors, *WS A-10-11*
value of, *WS A-1*
pictures. *See* images
planning
    community Web sites, *WS C-2-3*
    information Web sites, *WS D-2-3*
    online business Web sites, *WS C-2-3*
    small business Web sites, *WS B-2-3*
    travel Web sites, *WS E-2-3*
previewing
    frames, *WS E-8-9*
    Web pages, *WS A-4-5*
Publish button, *WS A-19*
Publish dialog box, *WS A-18-19*

►R

remote links
    creating, *WS A-16-17*
    defined, *WS A-8*
    finding and inserting, *WS D-12-15*
Remove All Styles button, *WS C-10*
Remove Link option, *WS B-18*

►S

Save As dialog box, *WS C-4*
Save Link As option, *WS C-6, WS E-4*
saving
    images, *WS B-4-5, WS E-14-15*

Web page files, *WS A-4*
Web pages under multiple file
    names, *WS B-2*, *WS B-6*
scrolling text banners, with JavaScript,
    WS F-18-19
search engines
    adding sites to, *WS A-18-19*
    meta-information and, *WS C-2*
    using, *WS D-14*
searching the Internet, *WS A-16*,
    WS C-4
    classification names and, *WS C-18*
    keywords and, *WS C-17*
security, JavaScript alert message,
    WS F-16-17
sizing
    frames, *WS D-9*
    images, *WS A-14*, *WS B-14*
small business Web sites, *WS B-1-19*
    alternate text and images, *WS B-16-17*
    counters, *WS B-18-19*
    developing pages for, *WS B-10-11*
    image editing in Paint, *WS B-14-15*
    images as links, *WS B-12-13*
    index page, *WS B-4-5*, *WS B-8-9*
    planning, *WS B-2-3*
    table of contents, *WS B-6-7*
    value of, *WS B-1*
sounds, JavaScript for, *WS F-18*
source code
    viewing, *WS C-18-19*
    for Web pages, *WS C-17*
special effects, with JavaScript,
    WS F-2, *WS F-18-19*
spell checking, *WS A-6*, *WS C-8*
    meta-information, *WS C-16*
Status bar, target name in, *WS C-15*
storyboards
    for community Web sites, *WS C-2-3*
    defined, *WS A-2*

for online business Web sites, *WS F-3*
for personal Web sites, *WS A-2*,
    WS A-3
for small business Web sites, *WS B-3*
for travel Web sites, *WS E-2-3*
Student Online Companion, *WS A-6*
styles
    heading, *WS A-4*, *WS A-6*,
        WS B-10-11, *WS C-8*, *WS D-4*
    removing, *WS C-10*
Submit button, for forms, *WS E-18*

►T

table of contents (TOC) page
    creating, *WS B-6-7*
    for information Web sites,
        WS D-6-7, *WS D-14-15*
Table Properties dialog box, *WS F-4-5*
tables
    alignment of, *WS F-4*
    backgrounds in, *WS F-10-11*
    border line width, *WS F-4-5*
    cell width, *WS F-4*
    color backgrounds in, *WS F-10*
    complex, *WS F-2*
    creating, *WS D-16-17*, *WS E-14-15*,
        WS F-4-5, *WS F-10-11*
    creating for interactive forms,
        WS F-12-13
    images in, *WS E-14-15*, *WS F-6-7*
    width of, *WS D-16*
tag icons, for targets, *WS D-10*
tags. *See* HTML code
targeted inks, creating, *WS C-12-13*
Target Properties dialog box, *WS C-12*
targets
    creating, *WS E-4*
    for frames, *WS D-10-11*

inserting, *WS C-12*
name, in status bar, *WS C-15*
taskbar buttons, ToolTips, *WS A-8*
text
adding to images, *WS B-14-15*
blinking, *WS C-10*
center alignment of, *WS A-10-11*
copying from other sources, *WS A-6*
enhancing, *WS A-6-7*
wrapping around images, *WS A-14-15*
text areas, adding to forms, *WS F-14-15*
text colors
links, *WS A-8, WS A-10-11, WS C-6, WS F-4*
selecting, *WS A-10-11, WS C-6, WS F-4*
titles, for Web pages, *WS A-4, WS C-6-7*
TOC. *See* table of contents (TOC) page
ToolTips, for taskbar buttons, *WS A-8*
travel Web sites, *WS E-1-19*
creating pages for, *WS E-6-7*
developing content for, *WS E-12-13*
forms for, *WS E-16-17*
frames for, *WS E-8-9*
image maps for, *WS E-10-11*
images for, *WS E-14-15*
links for, *WS E-14-15*
modifying HTML tags, *WS E-18-19*
planning, *WS E-2-3*
setting up, *WS E-4-5*
value of, *WS E-1*

URLs, ISPs and, *WS A-18*
users, greeting by name, *WS F-16-17*

viewing, forms, *WS E-18-19*

warning function, JavaScript, *WS F-16-17*
WebCrawler, *WS C-4*
Web pages
adding content to, *WS C-8-11*
developing, for small business Web site, *WS B-8-1*
meta-information for, *WS C-16-17*
previewing, *WS A-4-5*
saving under multiple names to create templates, *WS B-2, WS B-6*
source code for, *WS C-17*
storing and saving files, *WS A-4*
Web sites
adding to search engines, *WS A-18-19*
bookmarking, *WS A-16*
listing on "Best of the Web" sites, *WS C-19*
reviewing others, *WS C-4-5*
windows, memory requirements and, *WS A-12*

► **Y**

Yahoo, *WS A-16, WS A-18, WS C-4*